PSYCHOANALYTIC

PERSPECTIVES

ON MIGRATION

AND EXILE

Psychoanalytic

LEON GRINBERG

Perspectives

REBECA GRINBERG

on Migration

Translated from the Spanish by Nancy Festinger

and Exile

Foreword by Otto F. Kernberg, M.D.

Yale University Press *New Haven & London*

Published with assistance from the foundation
established in memory of Philip Hamilton
McMillan of the Class of 1894, Yale College.

Originally published as *Psicoanálisis de la
migración y del exilio*, © 1984 Alianza Editorial.

Designed by Richard Hendel
and set in Sabon type
by Marathon Typography Service, Inc.
Printed in the United States of America.

Library of Congress Cataloging-in-Publication Data
Grinberg, León.
    Psychoanalytic perspectives on migration and exile.
    Translation of: Psicoanálisis de la migración y del
exilio.
    Bibliography: p.
    Includes index.
    1. Emigration and immigration—Psychological
aspects. 2. Immigrants—Psychology. 3. Exiles—
Psychology. I. Grinberg, Rebeca. II. Title.
JV6109.G7513   1989   304.8   88-27951
ISBN 0-300-04011-3 (alk. paper)

The paper in this book meets the guidelines for
permanence and durability of the Committee
on Production Guidelines for Book Longevity of
the Council on Library Resources.

10 9 8 7 6 5 4 3 2 1

CONTENTS

FOREWORD

As far as I know, this extraordinary book is the first comprehensive psychoanalytic study of the psychology of emigration and exile. Here is a sophisticated treatment of adaptation, and the failure to adapt, to a new country, a new language, a new culture, written in a style at once elegant and simple. At its center is a study of normal and pathological mourning, essential constituents of migration and exile.

The book integrates two interlocking perspectives: first, the unconscious processes activated in the individual as he or she faces the challenges of leaving one world behind and adapting to a new one; second, the group processes activated by migration, both in fantasy and reality, especially among those who remain behind, vis-à-vis the émigré. These perspectives are in turn brought into relation to the broader social and cultural phenomena that influence an individual in transition.

Both authors are psychoanalysts of great distinction. León Grinberg is an outstanding theoretician, educator, and clinician, having pioneered with contributions to the study of group dynamics and group psychotherapy; he has also made original contributions in the clinical field in the area of identity, and persecutory and depressive anxieties. Rebeca Grinberg is an eminent child analyst whose rich clinical material adds to this book's value.

The Grinbergs have drawn on their knowledge of group processes, identity formation and identity diffusion, and on early and primitive psychopathology to describe the relations between parents and children who separate from each other, between those who leave and those who stay—the ambivalences, unconscious anxieties, and reparative processes involved in reencounters with the past.

Their book illuminates many phenomena usually taken for

granted because of their ubiquity but rarely studied. The Grinbergs penetrate the surface relations between those who migrate and those who remain. They describe the underlying guilt stemming, on the one side, from envy and resentment and, on the other side, from having abandoned family or friends or both. They also detail the defenses erected against these painful feelings, the regressive aspects of paranoid-schizoid, manic, and even confusional defenses against the pain of mourning. It would not surprise me if all those who have experienced migration either directly or indirectly were to find in this book an illumination of many experiences familiar to them.

Psychoanalytic Perspectives on Migration and Exile is a masterpiece of applied psychoanalysis and should be of particular interest to the psychoanalytic and psychotherapeutic professions as well as the educated reader of countries of immigrants such as the United States and Canada.

Otto F. Kernberg, M.D.

PREFACE

This book is the fruit of our experience. We have studied both directly, in private practice and hospital care, and indirectly, as supervisors and through interchanges with colleagues, the complex life experiences recounted by "transplanted" persons who have emigrated in various directions: from Europe to the Americas, from one country of the Americas to another, from the Americas to Europe, and from diverse parts of the world to Israel.

Each migration together with its "why" and "wherefore" is inscribed in the history of the family and the individual.

The psychoanalytic observations presented here were gathered in the three countries in which we have worked: Argentina, our country of origin, where we were educated and spent most of our lives; Israel, where we lived during different periods; and Spain, the country where we currently reside. In each of these countries we had the opportunity to analyze the vicissitudes of the migratory process in persons who had already emigrated as well as in persons preparing to emigrate. We would like to express our deepest gratitude to all those with whom we have worked.

Of course, our own experience as emigrants is not unrelated to our interest in the theme.

Madrid, 1982

INTRODUCTION

Human migrations are as old as mankind and have been studied
from diverse perspectives. Numerous studies have dealt with the
historical, cultural, demographic, religious, political, ideological,
sociological, and economic consequences of migration, which are
certainly of great significance. In recent years the subject has
begun to interest mental health professionals as well, by virtue of
the rising number of immigrants in need of counseling for psychiatric problems that may be directly traceable to migration.

Indeed, one cannot ignore the incidence of certain psychological problems particular to emigrants and those of their immediate entourage, in both the old and the new surroundings. These
problems are difficult to evaluate because the motivations for
migration and its consequences are closely intertwined.

At the outset one cannot help noticing that this subject has
been studied only cursorily from the psychoanalytic perspective,
despite—or perhaps because of—the fact that many pioneers of
psychoanalysis were themselves emigrants. Our intention is to fill
this gap by taking a closer look at certain phenomena which, if
systematized, would constitute a "psychopathology of migration."

We will begin by defining the scope of the term *migration* and
the various types of geographic displacements it covers: near and
far, temporary and permanent, voluntary and involuntary, and so
on. We shall go on to examine external and internal motivations,
as well as the expectations that color an individual or group decision to emigrate.

External factors greatly influence a person's predisposition to
migration, the nature of the migration, its possible consequences,
and the forms it takes. External circumstances being equal, the
personality of the individual, his prominent psychological traits,
and his age are factors that enter into the decision to emigrate or
not; and if one does emigrate, the same factors determine the

quality of the migration one undertakes. Personal or collective crises can cause migration, and the migration in turn may precipitate new crises.

We will take into account the interplay of emotional attitudes and reactions on the part of the emigrant and the people who make up the old and new environments. We will consider the emigrant's feelings toward peers (liberation, persecution, blame, loss, and so on) and the feelings of the peer group toward the emigrant (sorrow, resentment, blame, envy). The people among whom the newcomer settles may regard him as an intruder, thus rejecting him or treating him suspiciously, or they may view him with some measure of acceptance and hopefulness. In his relation to the new group, the emigrant's options, as identified by earlier writers on the subject, are "adaptation," "adjustment," or "assimilation." Although we do not dismiss these categories out of hand, our purpose will be to develop another perspective based on the qualities of the attachments between the newcomer and the receptor group. To a certain extent, these attachments are affected by the types of object relations the individual had before he emigrated and by the object relations of the community that receives him.

This study emphasizes the unique nature of exile. What sets exile fundamentally apart from other types of migration with their possible permutations and developments is that departure is involuntary and return impossible. Unarguably, exile, a result of civil wars and violence afflicting many nations of the modern world, is one of the most serious problems of our time.

In another connection we will look at the phenomenon of migration in terms of the different types of anxieties it can awaken: persecution anxieties in the face of change, the new and the unknown; depressive anxieties, which lead to mourning for the objects left behind and the lost parts of the self; and disorienting anxieties over the failure to distinguish between the "old" and the "new." These anxieties, together with the symptoms and defense mechanisms they may produce, are part of what we have called the psychopathology of migration. The evolution of this pathology depends upon how anxieties and feelings of uprooted-ness and loss are assimilated by the individual.

Last, but by no means of least importance, we will discuss the impact migration has on one's sense of identity and the crises it may precipitate. Such crises, as we shall see, constitute an exam-ple of what Bion calls catastrophic change; their denouement may lead to real catastrophe or just the opposite: successful, cre-ative development and its deeper significance, the enrichment of "rebirth."

1

MIGRATION AND MYTH

Myths possess a singular richness. Their images often transmit ideas more effectively than technical terms referring to specific psychological concepts. A myth may be compared to a mobile, multifaceted polyhedron which reflects different surfaces, angles, and ridges in the eyes of each beholder.

The effort it takes to understand myths and to discover what is hidden within them can be as great as that needed to find the latent significance behind the manifest content of the material in a psychoanalytic session. Some myths have had a great impact in the field of psychoanalysis, in particular with regard to their primitive content. The myths of Eden, Babel, and Oedipus illustrate and make more intelligible the conflict between those parts of the personality which seek knowledge and those which actively oppose this search. The conflict itself points up man's desire to "migrate," to go beyond fixed borders in search of knowledge, wherever it may lie, while at the same time man has a tendency to put obstacles in his own path (prohibition). By so doing, he transforms the "search migration" into an "exile-expulsion-punishment migration," which gives rise to pain, confusion, and isolation.

The first migration traces back to Adam and Eve. Impelled by curiosity (symbolized by the snake), they entered the forbidden zone of Paradise, where they found the tree that "was good for food, and pleasant to the eyes, and a tree to be desired to make one wise. . . . Eve took of the fruit thereof, and did eat, and gave also unto her husband. . . . And the eyes of both of them were opened"—they knew good and evil. Their transgression led to their expulsion/exile from Eden and from all the gratifications, safety, and pleasure Eden offered.

Exile, then, prevented the first human couple from gaining the deepest and most vital knowledge, that which endures throughout time and which is represented by the tree of life.

The Bible says that after expelling man and woman from Paradise, Jehovah "placed at the east of the garden of Eden Cherubims, and a flaming sword which turned every way, to keep the way of the tree of life." It is precisely this forbidding image of Jehovah and this model of punishment and obstruction in the way of true knowledge—the superego—that recurs in the narratives of the Babel and Oedipus stories.

These myths provide terms of reference to help us understand the difficulties facing the individual who attempts to bear the pain of true knowledge, "not only to know something, but to be that something"—to be oneself, with the actual effect of achieving mental growth and maturity.

In our view, the myth of Eden is also a symbol of birth—the first migration of human life, which brings about dissociation (knowledge of good and evil), emergence of the most primitive anxieties (paranoia and depression) caused by loss of the ideal object, and anxiety of the helpless ego left to fend for itself. "In pain shalt thou bring forth children": the pain of birth, of detachment; "by the sweat of thy brow shalt thou earn thy bread": the loss of the continuous, unconditional food supply via the umbilical cord and the need to search for one's own sustenance (the breast); the loss of object and consequent suffering (weaning), and the struggle to compensate for and rediscover the lost object: these are some of the "migratory" experiences man must pass through in his evolution, progressively distancing himself from his original maternal object.

Abraham the patriarch, father of nations, surrounded by his tribe and flocks, in leaving Ur, the city of his ancestors, severs his links with the idols worshipped there. Responding to the call of God he becomes a nomad; the God who created heaven, earth, and stars moves him to migrate in search of a new promised land in which to found a new people, "as numerous as the stars of the sky and the sand of the desert." Or so Abraham says.

Abraham's migration responded, in fact, to a need for a divinity more abstract than the divinity of idols, so that he could attain a deeper knowledge of the universe (the origin of heaven and earth). But, just as in the Eden myth, the desire to distance oneself from one's original objects in order to know and to create is punished by the same God who encourages it: he imposes the terrible condition that Abraham must be prepared to give up what is most precious to him, the life of his son, to be offered in sacrifice.

We also find several migrations in the legend of Oedipus: to prevent the Oracle's prediction from coming true, Oedipus's death sentence is commuted; he is sent on a migration that separates him from his real parents and his original peer group. His second migration occurs when, attempting to escape the Oracle's prophecy, he flees his adoptive parents' home and goes to Thebes. The third migration is his exile following parricide and incest. The myth of Oedipus, masterfully told in Greek tragedy, was elaborated by Freud and his followers in the theory of the Oedipus complex; they placed special emphasis on the sexual significance of the myth and the feelings of love, hate, jealousy, and rivalry the story contains. A historical parallel to the Oedipus myth can be found in primitive tribes whose totemic laws prescribe exogamic migration so that their members will not violate the taboos of parricide and incest.

The Oedipus myth has also been studied from another point of view, displaced by classic Freudian theory, with its emphasis on the sexual aspect. While not denying the importance of the sexual aspect, this other point of view concentrates on the link of knowledge, a link as vital to human experience as the links of love and hatred (Bion, 1963).

The riddle of the Sphinx was probably an expression of man's curiosity about himself, a curiosity also expressed in Oedipus's determination to discover the nature of his crime despite Tiresias's warnings to desist. (Curiosity has the status of sin in the Oedipus myth, as it does in the myths of Eden and Babel.)

Oedipus returns to Thebes to search for the truth. When he solves the riddle of the Sphinx, he acquires knowledge by conquering an image that is half-human, half-animal, a symbol of the combination of his parents, whose union arouses very archaic persecution fantasies. By defeating the Sphinx, Oedipus feels he has destroyed the unity of his parents, from whom, in his fantasy, he steals knowledge.

In the legend, one part of Oedipus undermines the determination of another part to persist in seeking the truth. Tiresias, who, significantly, has also been blinded because he saw the forbidden primal scene, tries to warn Oedipus not to proceed with his investigation. Tiresias symbolizes a dissociated aspect of Oedipus himself. The Oedipus story can thus be seen as an example of the conflict inherent in human nature between the impulse to steal the father's most valued and desired possession, exposing oneself to punishment and exile, and the repression of that impulse.

In classic Oedipal theory, the mother is considered the father's most valued possession and is the object of Oedipal jealousy and rivalry. The other approach to the Oedipus myth, and to the myth of Eden, holds that true knowledge, not the mother, is the object belonging exclusively to the father-God.

Moses, who led the exodus of an enslaved people to the land of freedom, and who dared ascend the summit of Mount Sinai to seek knowledge of the Law, was punished by not being permitted to set foot in the promised land: he was allowed to see it only from afar before dying.

Although not a myth but a historical reality, the voyages of Columbus offer another illustration of the strong human tendency to venture forth in search of the unknown. Despite the tremendous importance of his discovery of a new world, Columbus died in poverty, abandoned by his patrons and grief-stricken.

There seems to be a universal fantasy, variously expressed in myths and legends and children's stories of all eras, in which the satisfaction of curiosity, after a long and difficult journey fraught with dangers, confers great powers. This theme has been taken up in literature from *A Thousand and One Nights* to science fiction such as the fantastic voyages described by Jules Verne. But the satisfaction of curiosity is beset with dangers precisely because the fantasies to which it gives rise make it forbidden. The prohibition against true knowledge appears to have its origin in the seeker's inability to regard knowledge as a symbol; rather, the seeker tends to consider true knowledge as though it were actually an incestuous relation, taking literally the biblical expression "to know a woman" in the sense of having sexual union with her.

The blinding of Oedipus combines punishment for both sins: he loses his eyes as instruments which serve to satisfy his curiosity and as symbols of castrated sexual organs.

Exile converts the search for truth, a voluntary migration, into punishment and involuntary migration. In this transformation, the expulsion of Adam and Eve from the garden of Eden takes the work-birth-creation sequence (with the pain of detachment and the joy of childbirth) and replaces it with work-birth-punishment (pain as curse).

In the tower of Babel myth, the migratory impulse is expressed in man's desire to "reach heaven" so as to attain knowledge of "another world," different from the world he knows. But in this myth, man's desire is punished by the confusion of tongues and the loss of his ability to communicate.

An analogy can be drawn between the Babel story and the experiences of an immigrant who arrives in the "new world," a world totally different from the one he knows, where he encounters powerful internal obstacles to his integration into the new society—learning the language, adopting local customs and behavior, and so forth—with the accompanying danger of confusion and inability to communicate with others or with himself. These states of confusion may also result from the breakdown of effective defensive dissociation or from a premature search for integration which is developmentally not yet possible. Quite frequently the immigrant resorts to dissociative mechanisms—for example, idealizing all new aspects and experiences in the society that has taken him in while at the same time devaluing the people and places he has left behind, regarding them as persecutory. Through such dissociation he avoids the mourning, remorse, and depressive anxieties which would otherwise be aroused and intensified by the migration, especially if it was undertaken voluntarily.

Later, in our analysis of the quality of the bonds between the person who leaves and the group that stays behind, we shall describe in detail the emotional reactions and fantasies of each. Here it will suffice to say that every immigrant carries with him a mixture of anxiety, sadness, pain, and nostalgia, on one side, and expectations and hopes, on the other.

It is for the express purpose of protecting himself from the painful effects of these often intolerable emotions that the immigrant makes use of dissociation, so as not to evoke in a hopeless form the losses he has suffered: his beloved family, his lifelong friends, the streets of his town or village, the many objects of daily life to which he has grown affectionately attached, and so on. By belittling his losses, denigrating all that is known and familiar, and exaggerating his admiration for the new and unknown, he tends to negate his anxiety and guilt—feelings that are nearly inevitable in every experience of migration.

In other cases of migration, circumstances may evolve in such a way that the content of the immigrant's dissociation is inverted, and the respective values of each environment become reversed: the country left behind is endowed with every sort of magnified and nostalgic virtue, while the country of arrival is seen as full of defects and characterized by negative, persecutory connotations —this is the "disenchantment of the promised land."

It becomes essential for the emigrant to maintain the dissociation: good on one side, bad on the other, irrespective of which country represents either characteristic, because if the dissociation breaks down, the inevitable result is confusion and anxiety, with all its feared consequences: one no longer knows who is a friend and who an enemy, where one can succeed and where one must fail, how to distinguish between the useful and the harmful, how to discriminate between love and hate, life and death.

As we have seen, such confusion may be experienced as punishment for the migratory impulse, for the desire to know a new world . . . a different world.

2

MIGRATION AS TRAUMA

AND CRISIS

The title of this chapter may raise eyebrows, for some authors would define trauma exclusively as an acute phenomenon occurring over a short time span which produces psychological collapse when the mind is overwhelmed by the intensity of the stimuli besieging it.

Migration, although it extends over time, has an acutely traumatic phase; and it is our view that the notion of trauma should be applied not only to single, isolated events (for example, the sudden death of a family member, a sexual attack, unexpected surgery, or accident) but also to events which may be prolonged for greater or lesser periods, such as affective deprivation, separation from parents, residence in boarding schools or nursing homes, hospitalization, or migration.

The etymology of the term *trauma*, from the Greek, describes a surface wound accompanied by effraction, but the meaning of the word is not limited to its literal definition, since a violent blow of a physical or psychological nature, even in the absence of effraction, is considered a trauma. The term *traumatism*, on the other hand, is reserved for describing the consequences to the body of a violent attack from an external source. Psychoanalysis has taken the general sense of these terms and transferred them to the psychological plane: trauma is taken to mean any violent shock and its consequences to the personality.

In early studies (1895, 1896), Freud attributed the etiology of neuroses to past traumatic experiences, generally believed to have

occurred in infancy. The specific treatment techniques he pro-
posed were catharsis and the psychic working through of these
experiences. He held that psychologically what gave an event its
traumatic value were its particular circumstances: the subject's
special psychological condition at the time of the event, the subject's affective situation which prevents an appropriate reaction,
and finally, the psychic conflict impeding the subject from integrating into his conscious personality the experience he has
undergone.

In *Beyond the Pleasure Principle* (1920) Freud conceives trauma
as an excess of external stimuli which overcome the protective
barrier against overstimulation, leading to long-lasting disturbances in ego functioning. The ego attempts to mobilize all available strength in order to set up an anticathexis and thus to establish the working conditions for the pleasure principle to operate.
The existence of "accident neurosis" and "war neurosis" focused
Freud's attention on what he called "traumatic neurosis." He
attributed recurring dreams in which the subject relives the accident or has a tendency to place himself again in the traumatic
situation to what he termed the "repetition compulsion." Trauma
is not simply a disturbance of libidinal economy; it more radically threatens the integrity of the personality.

Later on, in 1926, the concept of trauma acquired a different
significance for Freud, quite apart from any reference to traumatic neurosis as such. The ego, he believed, sends out an "anxiety
signal" in its attempt to avoid being overwhelmed by catastrophic
"automatic anxiety," a frequent reaction to the traumatic situation in which the ego finds itself defenseless (disabled). This concept established a symmetry between internal and external danger:
the ego is attacked from within just as it is from without. Later
we will see how the experience of migration may produce phobic
symptoms or other manifestations of anxiety (insomnia, nightmares) as one way of using the anxiety signal in a measured and
controlled fashion: thus the individual avoids being swamped by
catastrophic anxiety.

One must be careful to distinguish between acute psychic

trauma—also called shock trauma—and other types of trauma, described by Moses (1978) as "tension traumas," "multiple traumas," "cumulative traumas," "silent traumas."

Freud himself pointed out (1895) that trauma may be caused by a single important event or by the accumulation of several partially traumatic events. Moreover, clinical observations of traumatic experiences would suggest that traumas should not be considered in isolation; rather, they occur in series. For example, the death of a father implies the mother's depression, a change in family structure and living conditions, the loss of the father's potential future contributions to the family, and so on.

Migration, similarly, is not an isolated traumatic experience observable at the time of departure/separation from one's place of origin or at the time of arrival in the new, unknown place where the person will settle. Quite the contrary; in any migration a constellation of factors combine to produce anxiety and sorrow.

These conditions may or may not show up clinically from the very beginning of the migratory process. An individual's reaction at the time of a traumatic event is not decisive in determining whether or not the event will have traumatic consequences later on: this will depend upon the subject's previous personality traits and other circumstances. It is even generally the case for there to be what is called a latency period of indeterminate length between the traumatic events and their detectable aftereffects, just as one frequently observes a delayed mourning period in cases of migrations.

We suggest, then, that migration as a traumatic experience comes under the heading of what have been called cumulative traumas and tension traumas, in which the subject's reactions are not always expressed or visible, but the effects of such trauma run deep and last long.

Pollock (1967) proposes that traumatic situations should be examined from the perspective of what he calls the three *P*'s: predisposition, precipitation, and perpetuation. That is, in the history of any subject there may be factors which, while not in themselves traumatic, may predispose the subject to respond traumatically to events that would not be traumatic to others. Such responses could be perpetuated if the subject were permanently exposed to recurring events, producing symptoms of chronic trauma.

Predisposition is important to consider in studying a person's response to traumatic situations, even to the most devastating traumas such as concentration camp experience. (Traumas have been studied in Holocaust survivors and veterans of combat.) Moses (1978) confirms this, maintaining that we always react to current events according to past childhood experiences, especially those having to do with loss of object, separations, and feelings of guilt. He compares traumatic situations to immunological reactions in which repeated exposure to the same type of trauma results in a propensity to act in an increasingly uncontrollable manner.

We believe that what characterizes a person's reaction to the traumatic experience of migration is the feeling of helplessness, which is modeled on the birth trauma (Rank, 1961), and the loss of the protective mother. It also corresponds to the experience of the loss of the "containing object" (Bion, 1970), which, in extreme situations, carries the threat of ego disintegration and dissolution and a blurring of boundaries. This risk is felt all the more intensely if the subject has suffered major deprivation and separation in infancy, with the resulting feelings of anxiety and helplessness.

Migration as Crisis

Generally considered an abrupt and decisive change in the course of any life process, crisis has been defined (Thom, 1976) as temporary disturbance of the regulatory mechanisms in one or more individuals. An individual or collective crisis can be either the cause or the effect of a migration. Every crisis implies the idea of "rupture," a separation or uprooting (Kaes, 1979). In growth crises there are times of deprivation and loss, as occurs in birth (the first crisis of a person's existence), weaning, the Oedipal crisis, puberty and adolescence, midlife crisis, and at the threshold of old age. Crises, be they developmental or set off by external or internal factors, are transition periods representing the opportunity for growth as well as the danger of increased vulnerability to mental illness.

Although Winnicott (1971) maintains that the continuity of existence is assured by cultural inheritance, the appearance of crises and their ruptures seems to show that cultural inheritance alone is not enough to ensure such continuity. This is equally true of crises that beset the adolescent, the immigrant, the farmer who moves to the city, and so on.

Winnicott considers "cultural inheritance" an extension of the "potential space" between the individual and his environment. A person's use of potential space is related to how he acquires "space between two"—between the ego and the nonego, the "inside" group (the group of origin) and the "outside" (receptor) group, between past and future.

The immigrant needs a potential space that he can use as the "transitional place" and "transition period" between the mother country/object and the new outside world: a potential space that grants him the possibility of experiencing migration as a game, with all the serious implications that games have for children. If he fails to create this potential space, the continuity between the self and the surroundings is broken. Such a rupture may be compared to that caused by the prolonged absences of an object needed by the child; as a result, the child loses his capacity to symbolize and must revert to more primitive defense mechanisms. A deprived child is effectively unable to play and exhibits an impoverished development of cultural awareness.

A deprived immigrant, through sustained loss of reliable objects in his environment, also suffers from diminished creative capacity. His ability to regain his skills will depend upon his capacity to work through and overcome this deprivation.

Migration is one of life's emergencies that exposes the individual who experiences it to a state of disorganization and requires a subsequent reorganization that is not always achieved. To some degree it is possible to predict the success or failure of a migration by evaluating the person's potential capacity to reorganize relatively rapidly after a temporary disorganization brought about by the anxiety of a stressful situation. In experimental interviews to identify personnel suited for assignment to specific jobs abroad, the candidate's capacity for rapid reorganization was judged to be a positive indicator.

In summary, we would suggest that migration is a potentially traumatic experience characterized by a series of partially traumatic events and at the same time represents a crisis situation. The crisis may trigger a decision to emigrate or, conversely, may reflect the impact of the migration.

If, because of his character predisposition or the conditions of his migration, the emigrant's ego is too severely damaged by the traumatic experience or the past or present crisis, it will be difficult for him to recover from the state of disorganization into which he has fallen, and he may suffer any one of many forms of mental or physical illness. If, however, he has sufficient capacity for working through, not only will he overcome the crisis but there will be a quality of rebirth to his recovery and a development of his creative potential.

3

THE EMIGRANTS

Those who emigrate and the conditions of their migrations are of an infinite variety. Since it would be impossible to include them all, we will describe particular cases which may serve as models for other situations. We are well aware that the life experiences of, say, a diplomat or a professor who moves frequently to new assignments far from his native land will differ greatly from those of an emigrant fleeing poverty in the hope of finding a place of refuge where he can survive. But careful comparison will reveal that there are common elements in the emotional reactions of all those who take part in migrations.

To begin, we must define the terms we will be using, above all *migration*. In general, *migration* has been used in its strict sense to refer to the geographic mobility of people who move from one place to another, whether as individuals, as part of a small group, or in a large mass.

It may be helpful to mention here past waves of mass migrations, in light of their important historical consequences. Among the earliest waves of historical significance was the westward migration of the nomad tribes of Europe and central Asia, which coincided with the fall of the Roman empire. Of perhaps even greater historical importance was the wave of European and African migration toward North and South America and Oceania, a flow that began shortly after the voyages of Columbus and in which it has been calculated that over sixty million Europeans traveled to other continents for reasons related to poverty, war, or epidemics, as well as to the need for human resources in sparsely populated regions. Unfavorable religious and political conditions also caused forced or mass migrations or both.

These great masses of people who became displaced at differ-ent periods for different reasons (economic, political, religious) headed for destinations that were considered or believed in fan-tasy to be the most hospitable. Beyond the external factors which justified their migrations, also at work was probably the uncon-scious fantasy of seeking a nurturing, protective earth-mother, a frequently idealized figure.

Migration proper—that is, a migration in which people come to be called emigrants of immigrants—occurs when the move-ment takes place from one country to another or from one region to another where the second is sufficiently distant and different from the first, for a sufficiently prolonged period of time such that one would consider the person as living in another country, there taking up the activities of daily life. This idea forms the basis for the definitions found in most studies of migration: the action and effect of moving from one country to another for the purpose of settling there.

The term *transplant* has frequently been used as a synonym for *migration*, though it contains the added nuance of being applied most commonly to individuals who are thoroughly rooted in their native environments; if forced to emigrate, they experience a most intense feeling of uprootedness—a feeling all immigrants experi-ence in some measure.

Although it does not fit squarely into the current definition, the move from a village to a big city, from a city to the country-side, from the mountains to the plains, and even, for some peo-ple, the move from one house to another could also be called a migration in the psychological sense.

The term *interior migrations* refers to displacements occurring within the same country. These moves may be definitive or tem-porary, to greater or lesser degrees, for reasons of work, study, and so forth.

It is important to differentiate between so-called foreign work-ers and immigrants. The former are, broadly speaking, persons who work temporarily in a country not their own but who retain the certainty of returning to their country of origin after a given period; the latter, by contrast, though it may (or may not) be possible for them to return to the place they came from, have decided to settle permanently in the new country.

The distinction between these two categories of people who leave their native lands is not purely semantic. For the former, "their thoughts are directed more to their return than to their departure" (Calvo, 1977). They know or suppose that their separation from their families or places of origin will be for a limited time, and this helps them to deal with the inevitable vicissitudes of experience in their new surroundings. The latter, however, experience a more marked sense of loss for all they have left behind, because they feel—rightly or wrongly—that the dissolution of ties is of a more definitive nature. Later on we will see how those in each category pass through periods of mourning, uprootedness, and attempts at adaptation, which may be successfully worked through or may result in psychopathological symptoms.

Finally, there are persons who are forced by circumstance to leave their countries and live elsewhere: they make up the great number of exiles, refugees, displaced persons, and deportees —people for whom a return home is out of the question for political, ideological, or religious reasons.

Generally, then, we may speak of voluntary and involuntary emigrants, categories to which we shall return later. This is a relative distinction, to be sure, since many emigrants who seem not to be forced to leave their homelands by external circumstance do so out of fear that sociopolitical or economic conditions may soon deteriorate to a point that would make their goals, life-style, or possibilities of subsistence untenable.

Involuntary migrations happen not only on an individual but also on a massive scale. Between 1947 and 1950, ten million people were forced by their respective governments to emigrate from Pakistan to India, and seven million from India to Pakistan, for religious reasons.

One must keep in mind that there also exist involuntary nonmigrations by virtue of laws of various countries restricting the entry or departure of emigrants. These create a situation in which people feel captive in a country where they would rather not reside, and they often take chances on illegal schemes enabling them to emigrate under dangerous conditions, with possibly dire consequences.

Sometimes, paradoxically, significant social change may result in migrations because of some people's resistance to change and their fear of the threatened loss of values, living conditions, and, in the final analysis, of those parts of the self which could be affected by the change. In these cases the individual does not dare to confront his primary fears—such as fear of losing established structures, fear of losing accommodation to prescribed social guidelines—fears which generate intense feelings of insecurity, increase his feelings of isolation and loneliness, and fundamentally weaken his sense of belonging to an established social group. Many people who emigrate for this reason tend to seek other places which, while they may be far away geographically, display social conditions and characteristics similar to those of the country of origin before the change took place. In these cases one may speak of sedentary migrations—an attempt to flee from the new and different in order to recreate and maintain without modification the known and familiar: to leave a place so as to be able to remain in the same place . . . to leave in order not to change.

Given its magnitude, the phenomenon of migration, which affects such a large number of individuals, has become, as Calvo (1977) remarks, yet another component of the way of life of our time. We would agree that however one tries to account for the phenomenon with sociopolitical or economic explanations, it remains a most serious problem for the individual living through the experience, and for this reason migration merits our close attention.

Some authors have looked to the psychological aspects of "emigrability" in an attempt to define the specific characteristics of those most prone to emigrate. For example, in 1959 Menges defined the concept of "fitness for emigration" as the potential ability to acquire gradually and comparatively rapidly in the new surroundings—provided that the new surroundings make it reasonably possible to do so—that measure of inner equilibrium which is normal for the person in question. By the same token, this person can become integrated into the new context without being disturbed or causing disturbances.

In addition, Menges posits "indications" and "contraindications" for emigration based on the person's ability to master or overcome homesickness. According to him, the danger of falling victim to homesickness is greater if the person has had limited success in his mental development toward individuation. Those who fall prey to homesickness usually have unresolved childhood problems arising from a conflicting relationship with the mother. In these cases it is more than a question of feelings of homesickness; it is rather a morbid dependency on the family establishment.

Stability of the marital couple and of the emigrant's family life is one of the factors that favors suitable migration, as are professional skill and job satisfaction. The same is true in the case of those who emigrate for ideological reasons, since they are less dependent on the external conditions of their place of arrival. On the other hand, those who have personal or family problems, lower on-the-job efficiency, or marked mental disturbances (as in the case of personalities which, because of the difficulties in adapting, become schizoid, paranoid, or profoundly depressed) could be expected to fail at coping with the impact of migration. Different types of family units can either facilitate or impede the possible migration of members. Thus, individuals belonging to family units described as agglutinated or enmeshed or epileptoid, which seem to swallow up their members (for whom separation is enormously problematic), will find it difficult to emigrate. On the other side, family units of the schizoid type seem to vomit out their members, who tend to distance themselves from one another and to disperse.

In general, when discussing the tendency to emigrate, we can classify individuals in two categories: those who need to be in constant contact with familiar people and places, and those who enjoy the possibility of being in unfamiliar places and forming new relationships.

In this connection, Balint (1959) coined two terms, "ocnophilic" and "philobatic," to describe, respectively, the tendency to hold onto what is certain and stable, and the tendency to seek out new and exciting experiences, situations, and places. Etymologically the terms are derived from the Greek words meaning "to grab hold of " and "to walk on one's hands" (like an acrobat).

Ocnophiles are characterized by their great attachment to people, places, and objects; they usually have a great many friends, and it is vitally important for them always to be near someone (not necessarily the same person at all times) who can offer help and understanding. They need objects, human as well as physical, for the simple reason that they cannot live alone.

In contrast, philobatics avoid ties of all kinds, tend to lead an independent life, and seek pleasure in adventures, voyages, and, above all, new emotions. They see human and physical objects as nuisances, and they leave them behind without pain or sorrow in order continuously to seek out new activities, new clothes, new places, new customs.

With regard to migration, it may be inferred, therefore, that individuals belonging to the first group are rooted in their places of origin and will leave them only with difficulty. On the other hand, those belonging to the second group have a tendency to emigrate in pursuit of undiscovered horizons and new experiences. They will seek out situations which satisfy three basic conditions: a goal that involves a certain degree of risk-taking; voluntary action to expose oneself to such a risk; and the expectation (sometimes omnipotent in nature) that they will overcome the danger. Neither of these categories, in and of itself or in isolation, constitutes an index of mental health. Perhaps what is most desirable is to achieve a good integration of both so that one can act in one way or the other according to one's evaluation of the circumstances.

In children's games, zones of security are called home and represent the mother. Many games and pastimes, such as amusement-park rides, include situations that awaken some fear (speed, for instance) to which the subject voluntarily exposes himself because he is fairly confident that he can tolerate and overcome the fear and afterward return to security. A mixture of fear, pleasure, and confidence in the face of danger is a component of all these games.

In our opinion, extreme attitudes in any of the basic categories described above activate pathologies which could be compared, at each extreme, to agoraphobia and claustrophobia, respectively. It is possible, for example, that some victims of the Holocaust became victims out of an extreme need to cling to the known, not daring to escape while there was still time. At the opposite pole, other people destroy themselves in a compulsive, uncontrolled search for new experiences: risky business enterprises, drugs, or constant, unjustified migrations of the manic type.

Some authors have variously identified the traits of what they believe is a preemigration personality; they maintain that schizoid personalities, who seem to lack a sense of rootedness, have a greater tendency to emigrate than other types of personalities. Others suggest that paranoid and insecure personalities, out of fear of persecution, continuously look for places they deem more secure than the place they are. In another interpretation, only persons with a strong ego and the ability to face risks will tend to emigrate.

One of the risks of migration is loneliness, something that everyone who emigrates will suffer from in differing degrees. The ability to be alone is one of the most important characteristics of maturity in emotional development, as Winnicott (1958) has pointed out. The individual acquires this ability in childhood on the basis of the skill with which he manages his feelings in relation to his mother, and after the triangular relationship has been established in relation to both parents. In other words, the child who feels excluded from the couple formed by his parents in the primal scene and who is able to master his jealousy and hatred increases his ability to be alone.

This ability has to do with the fusion of aggressive and erotic impulses, tolerance of the ambivalence of one's feelings, and the possibility of identifying oneself with each parent individually. For this ability to remain intact throughout the child's development and into adulthood, the individual will need to have good objects as part of his psychic reality. His relationship with these internal objects, together with the confidence they inspire and the integration he has achieved, will lay the foundation for him to be able to tolerate separations and the absence of familiar external objects and stimuli.

Individuals with good object relations will have a decreased tendency to paranoid reactions and a greater likelihood of projecting good internal objects onto the external world at the appropriate time.

The individual who has acquired this ability is in a better position to deal with the loss of familiar objects and the inevitable exclusion he will feel during the early stages of settling into a new environment. In his new life experience, his childhood feelings of frustration and exclusion in relation to the couple formed by his parents will be recreated, since the members of the new community have ties among themselves and share many things (language, memories, experiences, knowledge of daily life) in the new country to which he is as yet a stranger.

Melanie Klein (1963) has noted that the feeling of loneliness is based on an experience of incompleteness, which has its origin in incomplete personal integration. Also at work is the subject's conviction that some dissociated and projected parts of the self will never be recovered. This contributes to a feeling that he is not in full possession of himself and cannot feel that he belongs to any other person or group.

The possibility of developing a feeling of belonging seems to be a requisite for becoming integrated into a new country and also for maintaining one's sense of identity, as we have described elsewhere (Grinberg, 1971).

Persons in whom a feeling of loneliness with the above-mentioned characteristics becomes especially intense will find that their problems become exacerbated during migration because the migratory experience accentuates for a time the feeling of not belonging. One ceases to belong to the world one left behind and does not yet belong to the world in which one has newly arrived.

What kinds of people, then, emigrate? While we do not believe there is any specific personality type with a preconditioned tendency to emigrate, we do believe that there can be a greater or lesser predisposition to emigrate, linked to the factors set forth above and based on the constitution and history of each individual. Such predisposition may respond to various internal and external motivations and circumstances compelling the person, at a given time, to emigrate.

4

ANALYSIS OF A CASE IN

THE PREMIGRATORY PERIOD

PART I

In this chapter we will study the upheavals set in motion by external forces that affect one's sense of identity: we will consider a case history of a migration and its connection to disturbances of introjective and projective identifications. The analysis of Marisa, a patient treated by R. Grinberg (1965), will serve as an example.

The disturbances, and especially the obstacles to establishing good introjective identifications, were due in large part to significant migrations in the patient's past and to her lack of confidence in objects, which by their nature offered her few guarantees of stability.

Migration and the accompanying changes covering the wide spectrum of external object relations, made harder to bear in this case by their recurrence before the patient had worked them through, robbed her self of stability and as a result weakened her sense of identity. The prospect of yet another migration, which presented itself while she was in analysis, accentuated her difficulty in working out the multiple tasks of mourning. In addition, disorienting, persecutory, and depressive anxieties surfaced. The patient fell into regressive states, and her use of dissociative, omnipotent, and projective identification mechanisms increased. She exhibited a need to revert to psychopathic behavior via manic attitudes, though these were held in check by obsessive mechanisms.

Nearly all psychoanalytic definitions of identity state explicitly or imply that the development and consolidation of a sense of identity are based on assimilated introjective identifications. We know that these identifications derive from the interplay of introjective and projective mechanisms.

"A good object established in a secure form gives the ego a feeling of richness and abundance. . . . It is a precondition for developing an integrated and stable ego" (M. Klein, 1955). Stability enables a person to maintain continuity and sameness, which all authors agree are the defining traits of identity. Yet stability is also what makes it possible for each individual, though he may have certain traits in common with others, to be different from others—hence, unique.

Normal processes of individual development include a continuous working through of the many changes occurring throughout a lifetime: individuals must repeatedly suffer and accept the loss of previous stages of life by going through a mourning process, and they have to face the fear of the unknown in subsequent stages.

Migration is a change, surely; but it is a change of such magnitude that it not only puts one's identity on the line but puts it at risk. One experiences a wholesale loss of one's most meaningful and valued objects: people, things, places, language, culture, customs, climate, sometimes profession or economic/social milieu. To all these memories and deep affections are attached. Not only does the emigrant lose his attachments to these objects, but he is in danger of losing part of his self as well.

Since migration is a change that affects many of a person's attachments simultaneously, there is little likelihood that the less affected parts of the self can remain stable enough to support those parts of the self undergoing changes. Migration is an upheaval which shakes the entire psychic structure, and clearly, the less consolidated that structure, the more vulnerable it is to migration's aftereffects.

Yet there is no doubt that the conditions under which a migration takes place determine not only the predominant types of anxiety that will be mobilized but also their intensity, the defenses the subject erects against them, and the possibility of working them through.

Mourning the loss of one's homeland, after one has suffered persecution there, is different from mourning in a case of voluntary departure. In the former instance, paranoid anxieties are greater, while in the latter, depressive anxieties and guilt predominate. In each case, an infinite number of factors and situations give rise to unconscious fantasies about one's relation to one's own country (whether lost or left behind, definitively or temporarily) and to the "other country" (seen as threatening or seductive, persecutory or idealized).

We shall see how, in light of the concepts described above, these phenomena appeared in Marisa's migration story. Only material relevant to our theme has been abstracted from her clinical history.

Family Background

The reasons Marisa began analysis at the age of twenty, on the eve of her marriage, were directly linked to problems in the area of introjection, diffuse, hypochondriacal fears related to the oral-digestive tract, doubts about her impending marriage, fear of sexual relations, and a permanent state of anxiety.

Marisa lived in a perpetual climate of falsehood and deceit, which increased her distrust of objects and prevented her from knowing who she was and what properly belonged to her. Her father had left the diplomatic corps to set up a private legal practice. She did not know by what means he had acquired his wealth. The mother had given up an academic career when Marisa was born; a sister followed two years later.

The father had a violent temper. At times he receded into crises of melancholia with suicidal fantasies. The mother, very seductive, always seemed to be "hiding things." The patient, apparently the central figure of the family, was the mediator between her parents and between them and her sister during frequent family conflicts but was chronically physically ill.

Summary of Analysis up to the Premigration Phase

In Marisa's first contact with the analyst she displayed counterphobic behavior. She tried to act very self-assured during the interview, treating it as a very formal occasion. She briefly informed the analyst of her motives for seeking analysis. Dr. X. had referred her for treatment. She had initially gone to see Dr. X. out of alarm at her intense anxiety attacks and for fear that she was losing her mind over her wedding, which was imminent.

Marisa stated that she had not wanted Dr. X. to be her analyst because she preferred a female analyst, that she had gone to him only to obtain a recommendation. However, in her initial session, the first thing she said, commenting on the interview, was, "I was disappointed when I saw you. I imagined you as more masculine, with a tailored suit and dark hair pulled back, maybe in a bun." Later on we saw that she expected to find in the analyst the projection of her own physical image, identified with a phallic mother, through whom she could live out the fantasy of being analyzed by Dr. X.

Marisa herself wore her hair in a bun. Her head and hairstyle were themes that appeared regularly in the early period of her analysis, associated with frequent dreams in which analysis was represented by a beauty salon with the analyst as hair stylist who alternately tended or attacked the patient's bushy head, which sometimes symbolized a pregnant belly and sometimes an abundantly full breast.

This image had great significance because it was the physical expression of a basic transference fantasy in which the analyst was the mother with omnipotence of thought, physically represented by the head image, where the power of the father (Dr. X.) was concentrated. In this sense the erotization of thought and overvaluation of intelligence corresponded to an erotization of the relation between the nipple and the omnipotent breast (the bun), confused with a penis. She wanted to be analyzed by a woman, but by one who was masculine in appearance.

The transference relationship established from the earliest sessions (in which she projected onto the analyst various personalities from her childhood) signaled a double dissociation: high–low (mind–body) and good–bad (problems of spatial integration). The first image she projected onto the analyst was that of a doctor, which later alternated with that of the hair stylist. Her relation to the analyst as a doctor was a three-way relation involving Dr. X., who appeared as a dissociated part of the analyst. Dr. X. and the analyst represented two images of doctors from Marisa's childhood. She projected onto Dr. X. the image of the aggressive doctor who had mistreated her as a girl by pricking (injecting) her. The analyst, on the other hand, came to represent the kindly doctor who had cared for her occasionally and used to give her candy, but who had been dismissed by her parents because the "bad" doctor was the one who had gained their confidence.

The situation presented a very obvious Oedipal construct: in the patient's fantasy, the analyst was the kindly male doctor. But this seemed overly evident. She remembered that she had wanted to marry the good doctor, though he had a daughter her own age.

The appearance of this Oedipal material was premature and did not reflect the patient's real feelings. What she was really expressing were the persecution anxieties that she tried to keep at arm's length from the transference relationship. These anxieties were mobilized in relation to her marriage plans and her terror during intercourse of sadistic attacks by the bad father, who was experienced as a partial object, penis/injections, which she expected the analyst to counteract with a penis/candy.

When we look at Marisa's associations, the "illness" for which the doctors had been called, together with the fact that the doctors had come to be regarded as members of the family, we can appreciate the extent and intensity of her persecution anxiety at the deepest regressive levels and its relation to the maternal object.

Throughout childhood she had suffered various oral-digestive problems, mainly anorexia and chronic constipation, symptoms she still had upon commencing analysis. Her mode of retentive functioning was apparent in her reaction to the analyst's interpretations: she never referred to anything the analyst said in the session, nor did she acknowledge any interpretation until the following session, after having taken the interpretation home to examine in a safe place, out of the analyst's presence. Thus she manifested her food anxiety and her lack of confidence in anything her mother fed her—a result, as we shall see, of conflicts having to do with breast feeding and the extreme control she exercised over her sphincter to be safe from the possibility that her bodily contents could be forcibly removed. The existence of these fantasies in her past was confirmed by an extremely traumatic event which surfaced first as a highly confused memory. At the age of twelve—at a time when her father had just been posted abroad and his assignment changed several times, placing the family in a state of uncertainty—Marisa's disorders worsened while the family was traveling through a particular country, and as a result X rays of her digestive system had to be taken. She could not evacuate the "murky milk" she was given to ingest and developed a serious case of intestinal retention. A fecal bolus formed and had to be removed.

Marisa reacted with a severe dissociation between the country of origin (good milk) she had been forced to leave and the new country (bad milk), which took on persecutory characteristics. The bad milk represented barium, the "milk" she had to ingest so they could "see her insides" and expose her. Now the analyst was doing the same thing, trying to see inside her to discover what was there.

Furthermore, the incident of the masochistic retention of the barium probably indicated a depressive reaction to the loss of her native country.

But that was not her first experience of migration. For family reasons, her infancy also had been spent in a foreign country. She had been breast-fed until the age of two because her mother distrusted the food available in the "other country." At that time she was not anorexic; in fact, she was a plump baby. But along with the mother's milk she received—at an age when she needed other types of food—she absorbed the mother's paranoid fantasies, which contributed to the belief that "everything from outside is bad." This made her regress and idealize the breast along with anything that came from "inside." It was a breast that provided milk but little affective contact, perhaps because the mother was depressed on account of the migration. This could be deduced from several dreams which came up during analysis.

The other important aspect of the situation, one that weighed heavily on her ability to make introjective identifications, was the fact that part of Marisa's grade school education had taken place in her own country, but in an institution of a foreign community to which she did not belong, making her feel like a foreigner among her classmates. At the same time, the principal of the school was hired as her private tutor, since her father wanted her to learn the language of the country he was likely to be assigned to. She was "different" because she was the foreigner in relation to everyone at school, because she was rich (she was ashamed to show friends her ostentatiously luxurious house), because she enjoyed privileges (tutoring from the principal), and because at the slightest change in politics she could lose all these privileges.

The incident with the barium milk was linked in the patient's mind with menstruation and catastrophic fantasies of her insides being violently assaulted and robbed. Her mother referred to Marisa's menstruation as being "sick" and in general tended to encourage her daughter's hypochondriacal anxieties by suggesting frequently that she visit this or that doctor to see about some suspected illness. Her mother's attitude was a condemnation of her feminine sexuality: to be a woman meant to be sick.

Marisa expressed disgust at being a woman despite the fact

that she did the things she thought a woman "should" do: go to the beauty parlor, the dressmaker, and so on. She disdained these activities and showed respect only for intelligence and schooling. The value she placed on "the head," seat of the mind and of the highly prized intellect, contrasted with the contempt she showed for her own body.

Her mother seemed to be an insignificant figure for the most part, but when she was mentioned for the first time in analysis, it was in connection with the words "disgust" or "disillusionment."

It was clear that Marisa was ashamed of her mother's coarseness, despite an outward refinement, and that Marisa's anorexia was related to oral sadism, against which she defended herself with a reaction-formation, like her mother, who did not eat meat. But this refusal to eat also signified damage, because in her fantasy her mother equated meat with the despised father's penis. Marisa's disgust and intolerance toward food and toward the analyst's interpretations expressed a sadistic and derogatory oral fantasy about the penis.

During the time that this material was being worked through, while Marisa's psychic conflicts and problematic relations to the outside world were being uncovered and presented to her, her constipation began to improve and there was a slow improvement of her anorexia.

With regard to her fiancé, her choice of object is better understood in the context of her past, as described above. She and Ricardo were natives of the same country, but they had met abroad. In one sense her object choice was based on a paranoid attitude, since in her projective identification with her mother, she mistrusted "foreign men." Even so, she chose someone who was in one sense "foreign" to her family—they were practicing Catholics, an important factor in their social standing, and she fell in love with a Jewish man.

In sexual relations, which Marisa had counterphobically and compulsively initiated, she was frigid. Sex caused her intense anxiety. In the early stages of analysis she dreamed that she and her fiancé were discovered in the act, or that "it showed on my face."

The beginning of genital activity, which marked a new aspect of her sexual identity, caused such anxiety as to make her feel that her whole identity was endangered. It was not just that her face would give her away, that everything she felt guilty about would be discovered, but that she would cease altogether to be herself and would have a different face (Greenacre, 1958).

Both her sexual relations and her subsequent marriage appeared to be acts of rebellion against her father, attempts to leave him out of decisions which, in her view, he would only oppose. She could separate herself from him only by being "against." A family argument ensued, her father relented and accepted her choice of marriage partner, and then he began lavishing her with gifts which she could not enjoy because she felt that they came with too many strings attached. She felt that her umbilical cord had never been cut and that she could not separate what others had given her from what was rightfully "hers" (introjective identification, or internal object links that become part of the self and contribute to the sense of identity). In the same way she felt the analyst would always take back her interpretations, because they belonged to the analyst alone.

Yet, despite her protests that her umbilical cord had not been cut, her chief worry about her marriage was a paranoid fear of impoverishment, expressed in terms of money. She would lose her family, be "poor and alone" and at the mercy of her husband (the bad doctor who sadistically injects her and removes her bodily content). Actually, her new status and new home were for her "another country" and marriage yet one more migration. It is important here to understand that her migratory experiences contributed to her persecutory anxieties at a time when she was changing her life and taking on new roles.

Analysis of this material enabled Marisa to face marriage without severe anxiety crises some months after the date originally fixed. From then on, she felt more at ease in analysis, although communication remained problematic. The sessions were punctuated with long silences, and she continued to carry the analytic interpretations home with her to "think over."

Postmarriage

When Marisa attempted to reestablish the links with her family that in her mind had been broken when she set up housekeeping elsewhere, her psychopathic mechanisms were activated. This behavior was her response to migration, an attempt to regain the objects she was at risk of losing and for which she could not mourn. Her psychopathy began to operate as a defense against depression.

She was constantly provoking arguments with her husband over trivial matters while continuing to be "reasonable" with her parents and conciliatory in disputes between them. Through self-aggrandizement she exaggerated her importance in these situations, saying that they made her feel alive. In all probability she was subtly provoking these confrontations while denying that she played any instigating role, a dynamic first discovered during analysis.

In her sessions, Marisa was eager to make an impact and create surprise. She would say something like "Something incredible happened to me . . . ," followed by a long pause by which she was attempting psychopathically to manipulate the transference relation by building suspense and arousing the analyst's interest so that the analyst would become dependent on her and hang on her every word.

Studying became difficult for her; she could not concentrate and set herself up in impossible rivalry with her husband, who was working and at the same time attending university. While she firmly denied any such rivalry, she projected her persecution beliefs onto the interior decorators who had just redone her house and onto the maids, even though she was overly trusting by leaving jewelry and other valuables within their reach as though to tempt them.

Faced with the fear of losing her intellectual stature and disdaining her role as wife, she remedied the situation by becoming a mother.

The Child Fantasy

The immediate prospect of having a child calmed many anxieties from a variety of sources. Marisa had a manic, urgent need to fix things and deny the emptiness inside her by consolidating her identity in a maternal role. This assuaged her fear that her husband had emptied her intellectually and financially and had failed to give her anything in return. It concealed the intellectual failure connected with her schoolwork—extremely painful for one who had always been a brilliant student. Furthermore, she had a messianic fantasy regarding her future child: it would unite the couple and allow her to achieve orgasm. In this sense her frigidity distressed her when she experienced it as something missing physically because it prevented her from integrating her body image into her identity: it was a part of her body that she did not possess. The excitement she felt when involved in family arguments substituted for erotic stimulation and meant to her that she was "living" in close proximity to her possessions. It was her way of winning the competitive relationship with her husband. Finally, the child became a way to renew her dependency on her parents, creating more serious financial problems for her and at the same time placating her parents. She said, "Papa will have to support him and Mama will have to look after him, because I will have to study."

Detailed analysis of these fantasies caused her to reconsider the urgency of her wish to become pregnant and allowed her to resume classes and accumulate some credits. But during the first holiday break in the analysis, she did become pregnant. Clearly, she could not tolerate separation without reverting to a manic reaction, and then she acted like a thief by withholding the information from the analyst for several sessions.

Pregnancy

Consistently, the central theme of Marisa's analysis was her need to defend herself from the persecutory mother who, as a figure in several dreams, was trying to steal her baby from her. At times this image was projected onto the transference relationship; at times the analyst was seen as the permissive mother who protected her from the bad mother. Maternity did not fulfill Marisa; because of the constant presence of a persecutory mother who threatened to empty her, maternity did not belong to her. In some of her dreams her wish was to have a daughter, who represented Marisa herself as well as her sister, to whom she was very attached.

The sessions began to be dominated once again by Marisa's hypochondriacal preoccupations, but these were presented for their shock value, to see if the analyst reacted as the mother did. With the analyst's interpretive responses, her symptoms disappeared rapidly.

The birth was normal; Marisa followed training instructions and had a painless labor. Given her history, fetal retention might have been feared, but she merely complained to the doctor that he had, in her opinion, taken the baby out too quickly.

It was very difficult for her to separate herself from her newborn daughter; she considered the baby a part of herself and tried, through her, to reinforce her own identity. She had deeply loving contact with the baby from the start, but it was difficult to distinguish her caring from overprotection and a denial of separation.

Breast-feeding

During the breast-feeding period, a change took place: the persecutory image of the mother was projected onto her father and husband; in the transference relation, she assigned paternal characteristics to the analyst. "Men" and "analysts" appeared repeatedly as "madmen and thieves" (madness was experienced as theft) in a wide range of contexts.

At the same time she asked her mother to help care for her daughter, although Marisa was always in control of the situation, never leaving her daughter in her mother's hands unattended.

What was most significant was the type of relation Marisa had with her daughter: ideal and unconditional, a relation in which the husband was not permitted to participate. She kept her contact with the outside world to a minimum, and likewise her sexual contact, for, she said, "I couldn't do that to the baby." She discontinued her studies—finally, according to her—belittling the career she had once valued so highly. She could set aside the "omnipotent head" as long as she possessed the "omnipotent breast." Her obsession with the child went beyond the naturally close mother-child relationship of early infancy; it was an autistic attitude toward the outside world, from which she tried to withdraw by forming a symbiotic union with the child.

Weaning

One session began with the dramatic announcement, "My milk has dried up and I've begun menstruating. It's horrible to see my breasts like this; before they were firm and full, now they're soft, droopy, as though they were dead" (catastrophic weaning, in which the birth of her child and her own birth are relived). "I feel like it's over with you as well. I'd like to give you a nice present but I can't; I have no money."

By this time her daughter was seven months old and had begun teething. The pediatricians had advised her to change to solid foods. Marisa was inconsolable; she could not get over this separation and saw the loss of her breasts (identified with the weaned baby) as an internal emptying (loss of milk and menstruation) which left her "dead," unable to make reparations ("no money"). During this period her dreams became sinister and contained many variations of her fantasy of being torn limb from limb.

The assimilation of this material was an important landmark in Marisa's analysis because in the midst of frustration and change, she managed to avoid reverting to the usual hypochondriacal and psychopathic mechanisms and was able to reestablish more positive contact with the outside world.

Her relationship with her husband underwent a profound change, and their sexual relations became more satisfying. Her rivalry with him subsided and she was able to resume school-work. She not only obtained good grades, she also became more interested in her field of study. The joy of learning itself became more important to her than grades.

Her greatest achievement was to be able to study without developing an illness (her old dissociation of mind and body) or abandoning her roles of wife and mother, parts of her identity which she allowed to maintain their respective functions.

The fact that she could study and have sex without these activities being mutually exclusive stemmed from the fact that she had worked through the various implications of the predicament expressed in the "weaning dreams." She came to see that in her desire to dismantle her mind so as to save her body (that is, in sacrificing what she saw as her masculine side—identified with her student-husband—to save her feminine side—her breasts and belly) she was at the same time sacrificing her sexuality, because her husband was not only a student but her sex partner as well, and in cutting him off she was cutting off the sexual part of her-self connected with him.

She was able at last to let the maid prepare the baby food and baby-sit in her absence without falling prey to feelings of disgust or fears of infection or poisoning. Her anorexia improved and her figure developed (after giving birth she had become very thin). She also stopped wearing her hair in a bun (false identity—omnipotent breast).

Just as she began to allow the maid to do the cooking, she also began to allow the analyst to "cook up" interpretations, and she was not afraid to "digest" them, accepting them as belonging to the analyst. This showed that her relation to her analyst, the container of her projective identifications, was sufficiently well established for there to be a glimmer of hope that she would accept the analyst as a nourishing breast from which she could introject the sustenance that would fill the void inside her.

5

ANALYSIS OF A CASE IN

THE PREMIGRATORY PERIOD

PART II

The precarious equilibrium Marisa had achieved was seriously jeopardized when the possibility of another migration presented itself. Her husband obtained an attractive job offer with excellent future prospects, but the job was in another country. This situation refueled Marisa's anxieties about her identity. She felt empty when faced with the loss of her familiar roles.

The possibility of migration represented a threat of disintegration. She had recently begun to fulfill more than one significant role at the same time without feeling that they were mutually exclusive. She was aware of beginning to achieve integration in her life. When the new situation arose there existed a danger that she would turn it into a catastrophe because it exacerbated her schizoid mechanisms in such a way that in her mind it reactivated her predicament in previous migrations.

The objective of analysis at that juncture was to strengthen her introjective identifications so as to prevent projective identifications from robbing her of her ability to function. The aim, in other words, was to get the patient to reintroject all the projected and dispersed parts of herself. Thus she would be able to recognize the decisions and objects that were hers. Only then would the motivations behind any decision she made become clear —motivations setting in motion her maniacal mechanisms as well as those tending toward reparation. Finally she decided to accompany her husband abroad.

Coping with migration meant facing the simultaneous loss of many objects and bonds, the loss of a familiar environment and language, and the need to summon up enough flexibility and stability to build a daily life in the new country. All this required that Marisa grieve the multiple losses and recover the libidinal object energy that she would need to form new bonds. At first the new job offer and the separation it might entail were brought up in analysis as fantasy, nothing more. Later it became an idea with a slim chance of realization, and finally it became a real situation in which Marisa suddenly felt involved.

A number of themes were analyzed as they came up. In the first place, her rivalry with her husband resurfaced; she thought that now that she had resumed classes on a regular basis and was successful he could not tolerate her success and was trying not only to further his own career but, what is more, to obtain a most desirable, highly competitive position.

On another level, however, her husband represented herself. It was she who could not tolerate her recent successes. She looked for a way of escaping the increased responsibilities that success brings, as for example when she said, "Now that I can get down to studying, I have to stop going to school."

In the transference relation, a possible migration meant that Marisa could avoid dealing with her fantasy that she had taken from the analyst all her valuables, thus laying herself open to punishment and retaliation. On the other hand she was also fiercely trying to establish her independence from her father. By moving she would show him she did not need him. At the same time she would be acceding to his wishes by moving back to the country where he had sent her to school as a child. She wanted to achieve independence but could not accept the idea that her sister would remain at home, taking Marisa's place and dislodging her completely from the family.

This illustrates one aspect of her identity problem: she could not take on any role completely because she believed she would automatically lose any previous roles she had fulfilled and would lose continuity of herself over time (social, temporal, and spatial integration links). At a more regressive level she felt she could not give up the breast without risking the loss of her mother because her sister was inside the mother's uterus.

The impact of the new job offer and of the impending move was examined in analysis. She experienced these as implying the loss of her role in the family and of her place in analysis: she was afraid of confusion and entertained death fantasies in which she was killed and replaced by her sister. After this stage she tried to refortify her defenses. For some weeks she engaged in a full-fledged "flight from reality"—she threw herself into activity, laid out plans for the future, studied hard, and passed an exam.

It seemed as though everything in her life was answering Marisa's need for reassurance. She decided between two possible cities of destination, opting for the one that "wasn't too cold." Around this time, she interjected during one session: "Do you know that my midwife had a patient die on her?"

From that time on her anxieties reappeared with great intensity. She fantasized the prospective separation as castration, weaning, and birth—situations involving the danger of death: migration for her was going to be a "catastrophic birth."

In the months that followed, her fantasies revolved around her attempts to reestablish an idealized relationship to the breast or to her mother's interior, where the penis had been: She was going to abandon her studies, have a child, a son, in the new country, and enclose herself with him in an ivory tower; she would not need sexual relations, would not go out, and thus would not need to speak another language. These fantasies served a double purpose: first, through them she expressed her hostility toward her husband, the new country, and the analyst. She experienced the analyst as her husband's mate: they were the parents who tried to wean her so as to make room for another daughter. Second, her fantasies presented an experience opposite to the one she actually had, of being "wrenched out from inside," synonymous with death. She fantasized about being pregnant in the "other country."

In response to increased persecutory feelings, she sought refuge in a manic regressive state in which she libidinally invested the image of an internal, idealized object.

Recalling an earlier migration, during the period of her lactation, when her mother's paranoid attitude perpetuated breast-feeding to guard against the "poison food" in the other country and she was dislodged from the breast because of her sister's gestation, now she was afraid that her sister would take her place and leave her exposed to the dangers of the other country. To deal with the anxiety of the unknown, she tried to act in fantasy as her mother had acted in a similar situation.

Yet the risks she foresaw in her regressive fantasy were far from negligible. In thinking about having a second child, she recalled how she had felt when her daughter was born. Although she had tried to deny her anxiety by saying "things would have turned out the same even without analysis," she added later: "Sometimes I get scared when I think about how I was then and to what extent I felt I was living outside of time. Actually, I think that if it wasn't for analysis I would have lost my mind after giving birth."

Her regression represented a danger which she sought to counteract through forming a bond with someone who symbolized her father. She had plans to go into a "fabulous business" with a man, involving merchandise from a dubious source, but she would have to invest everything in the business, thereby "emptying herself" of all she had achieved.

Around the time she became involved with this person in a business fantasized as some sort of "sex affair," she became frightened by a homosexual, regressive, sadistic fantasy about the analyst which appeared in her dreams. Gangs of young hoodlums killed a woman who kept a lot of bottles, and Marisa was locked up with this woman.

The way in which she established a relationship with the male business partner is full of significance and illustrates the workings of projective identification. Her increased persecution anxiety, brought on by what was lacking (hunger/migration) in her life, was another factor that inhibited introjective identification and promoted her reliance on projective mechanisms (Klein, 1955).

One session during this period began,

> I was going completely out of my mind. Inés [her daughter] was hungry yesterday and the maid didn't have her food ready, because I've been busy studying, and if I'm not on top of everything, nothing goes smoothly. The baby began to whine. I was very upset by this and two big drops of milk fell from my breasts. [silence] And something else: I was thinking about Z. [the potential business partner]. It seems he has everything, but he's looking for a partner. Sometimes I look at him, I don't know, I just look at him. I thought about how I would feel if I were him. He knew I was looking at him. At first he seemed nervous and dry, then he relaxed. I'm ashamed to be telling you about such an adolescent incident.

The baby's fear of being left alone to die of hunger made a strong impression on her. That was why she felt she had to rely on the omnipotence of her breasts and nipples, which were supposed to provide drops of milk in emergencies. She also attempted to possess an omnipotent penis in order to use its ejaculation at any time, which was why she tried to put herself in Z.'s place ("if I were him"). Meanwhile, she had tried, by her look, to project this hungry part of herself onto him ("he's looking for a partner").

She continued: "He really looks like Papa. It was the first thing I noticed, and he has light eyes like the baby, and like you." Although this episode seemed to be an acting out of the Oedipal fantasy, on another level she was trying to construct, through Z., a fantasy of self-sustenance. To avoid frustration, she needed omnipotent nipples for permanent milk flow, or she needed an omnipotent penis, which she tried to obtain through projective identification with a man. The intensity attached to the projection made her feel that her identity was shaky and that she was losing her mind.

Moreover, by regressing she not only denied the passage of time but also attempted to control future time by doing away with the intolerable waiting period before her departure: Z. came to represent the "other country" and was idealized so as not to be feared ("fabulous business").

Her relationship with Z. was also, for reasons that cannot be gone into here, an attempted regression to adolescence and to being Daddy's girl. In this way she manifested her need to regain before she left a part of her life she had missed because of her hurried and counterphobic marriage. Back then, she had escaped the future by going forward (one might say, claustrophobically); now she was afraid of what lay ahead and wanted, agoraphobically, to escape by going back.

It was not surprising that she needed to return to her adolescence, the time of life's major identity crisis with regard to physical changes and changes in the image of one's parents.

Marisa had been unable to get beyond that stage. In adolescence the baby girl appeared again, the girl who belonged to the gang, the girl who killed her mother to separate her from the father. In this sense Marisa experienced leaving the country as a way of escaping from the analyst to marry her father, leaving the analyst alone and without a mate.

Her regression to childhood situations of perverse and sadistic dissociations was reminiscent of dreams she had had while weaning her daughter, dreams in which a gang of adolescents carved up a married couple in the attic.

Thus we see that the anxiety of a new separation caused her to react by using the same model of catastrophic response as she had to weaning: the regression to oral-sadistic fantasies played out by various dissociated parts of herself, the gang of toughs.

In this attempted acting out, the parts of Marisa that dissociated from the transference relation were her infantile female part (the hungry baby) and her masculine part (the omnipotent penis).

Feminine Identity

Marisa's feminine identity could not be sustained by the narcissistic hunger fantasies. They prevented her from moving toward a positive resolution of her Oedipal problem.

Her hunger, brought on by the prospect of migration, drove her next to become enmeshed in gender conflicts. Once again she became engaged in rivalry with her husband and with men in general: "Papa wanted to give me money. He treats me like a mistress now: he doesn't want Ricardo to know; all he needs to do next is give me a mink coat. . . . Lately things haven't been good with Ricardo again. The baby must have something to do with it: she wakes up at night and cries, calling to him, and she says, 'Mine, mine.' She pronounces it well now. The other day she said that Daddy was bad because he didn't want to put the candy in there, and she pointed to her vagina."

The patient's possibilities of consolidating a feminine identity were undermined. Her relation to the reality in which she had a feminine role to play was affected by two factors: (1) her mother did not serve as a good role model of a mature, sexual woman —"everything that comes out of Mother is false"—and (2) her father may have preferred to encourage a perverse type of relationship (the mistress) or have encouraged Marisa's childhood masturbatory inclinations ("studying as distraction").

The deficit in her feminine identity engendered the fantasy of having an omnipotent penis in her mind with which she could control her father. The same early Oedipal frustration aggravated the oral-sadistic impulses located in a hungry vagina which wanted to possess the object ("mine, mine") in order to keep it.

Marisa's weakened feminine identity led her to engage in a kind of infantile sexuality with perverse tendencies, which fulfilled her Oedipal fantasies.

When summer vacation and the time of separation drew near (for her, the first act of the major separation still to come), she repeatedly, even desperately, spoke of feeling out of place, of having nowhere to study, of wandering the streets because "all the bars were closed and there wasn't even a place to sit down." One reason she felt lost and unprotected was that she had to do without the sustenance of analysis. These feelings also expressed a greater anxiety regarding her upcoming trip and her dependence on and hunger for the analyst, which was difficult for her to recognize.

Logically, her separation from analysis during vacation meant that she would have to confront all the anxiety related to her scheduled migration. It is important here to note the way in which she tried to protect herself from intolerable emotions: dependence and hunger.

Her refusal to admit an oral dependence on analysis became clearer later. The closed bars (vacation from analysis) this time reflected what had been her internal psychic reality during the entire premigration period: the inner "bar" was closed even while she had been undergoing analysis, because she could not form an introjective identification with a breast that had "good milk." She could not believe that the analyst valued her unless she thought of it in terms of the analyst needing her badly; and she thought that if she ever returned from her migration the analyst would not recognize her: with her departure she would cease to exist, she thought, in the mind of the analyst.

Her feeling of "not receiving" did not relate to material things or the breast that did not give milk; it arose from the fact that she had not felt any real affectionate contact: "everything about Mother seems false." She dressed her analyst in the same maternal image; the analyst only cared for her "for money": omnipotent fears that could attack, conquer, pacify, or feed on themselves.

The fact that the analyst did not actively oppose her leaving was interpreted by Marisa as meaning that the analyst did not need her and did not care whether she stayed or not. This meant, among other things, that she "did not exist," had lost her identity. She believed she was a "nobody," that she did not matter.

She also had to reverse this situation in order to feel omnipotent; for when she was in great need and did not get what she needed she felt she did not exist. According to Bick (1965), when a child cries and the mother does not come, the child feels diminished and feels as if he does not exist for the mother.

Thus Marisa reverted to pathological introjections of "strong figures" (her analyst was going on vacation); then, by means of projective identifications she tried to control these figures sadistically and omnipotently. But in her psyche these figures intermingled with different aspects of (total and partial) object relations. She became confused, unable to tell good from bad, suffered a serious identity disturbance (madness), and risked ruining her good relationship with the analyst (father-figure) because of aggressive actions originating in that part of her associated with bad objects.

The Glass Identity

After the vacation break Marisa's dissociation reappeared in various guises, especially in her reference to "the baby." In this way she could control the two objects simultaneously, the new, unknown "other country" and the country of origin. This came up in one session when she mentioned that her daughter had discovered that she could see in the windowpane both the furniture in the room and the street. In the window, the armchair was both "inside" and "outside."

An analysis of this material suggests that Marisa wanted to feel like the armchair, to be inside and outside at the same time. That is, she wanted to be able to be in two places at once. In this way she was trying to negate in an omnipotent way the separation, loss, and trauma of the migration. Still, her basic fantasy was to identify with the windowpane, in which other objects are reflected.

She saw the analyst's role in a similar light; the analyst should be a screen for patients and not have a separate life. Mother and father existed for her only when she could see herself in them. Yet even so, the analyst as screen was not trustworthy; the image of herself that the screen returned was confused with what was visible on the surface. It was a permeable screen that devoured her identity. For Marisa to feel that she was made of glass was an expression of her lack of identity and her sensation of being emptied of her own possessions: "Everything I'm about to say I think is borrowed from Ricardo. It's either something he is interested in or some influence of yours [the analyst]. Then I feel totally empty. I could assume anybody's form, I could be XX.'s wife. I remember the movie *The Woman and Her Husbands*—I feel as though I were a nobody."

The material from the movie explained how she used her objects as repositories of everything she could not tolerate; yet she also invested in them everything she considered valuable, thus emptying herself. For this reason she fractured her objects into many parts (many husbands) to spread out the danger of her projections and reduce the danger of introjection.

The negated aspect of this material was that, in the movie, all the woman's husbands suffered the same fate: she made them rich (brought them luck) and then they died. Marisa felt that she had made the analyst (and her husband) rich. But her fear of killing the analyst was so strong that she could not assume any responsibility for what occurred in the analyst-patient relationship. Everything was done with "Daddy's money," of which she was simply the carrier, as was her mother: a windowpane in which no trace of a reflection is found.

As the date of her departure drew nearer her depressive anxieties became so intolerable that her need to escape again into dissociation and projective identification intensified. The last period of her analysis marked the height of her regression. She attempted to treat her departure as a repetition of earlier migrations in which she had been a passive player. She had submitted to them, been transported. She had taken no part in the decision whether to leave or to remain.

All this became most noticeable when she had to begin planning for her departure in earnest. She was about to move and thus had to assume some responsibility for her movements.

As it developed, moving had a deep association for her with

intestinal movement; that is, it represented leaving behind her constipation, one aspect of her inner paralysis. It also signified the risk of moving her feces—experienced by her as concrete aspects of her self which would be scattered about, exposing her again to emptiness. She did not want to confront any part of whatever could cause pain. Her apartment had to be leased or sold, and she did not want to show it to prospective tenants so as not to suffer over it. She would leave the flat and let her husband be the one to show it to strangers.

Such was her attitude toward her inner situation as well, as was brought out by interpretation of her material: in order not to suffer over what she was leaving behind, she refused to see what it was that truly belonged to her. In addition, she projected onto her husband everything she had denied internally: to have things, to want to leave so as to acquire more, and to suffer over leaving and losing other things.

By forcing her husband to show the apartment she was dissociating and projecting her suffering onto him, putting him in a position similar to that of a younger brother being thrown out of the house. Possibly because her sister was born around the time that Marisa was being weaned, she now tried to leave home in a manic manner, depositing in a brother figure the part of herself that was being evicted, as well as the part of herself that experienced claustrophobic anxieties.

These brothers also represented the possible analysands who would take her place when she was gone. She had found out that some people she knew had approached her analyst—although the analyst's work load did not permit her to accept them as patients. This was a source of great pleasure to Marisa because she had someone on whom to project her feelings of eviction, and she protected herself from jealousy toward the person who would occupy her time slot in analysis by voicing her opinion about the applicants she thought the analyst should accept for treatment. Yet she could not help but have strong feelings of envy at the thought that the analyst could have other "children." In her eyes, then, she, Marisa, would lose all value of her "own."

Her analysis during this period focused on some very rich dreams that provided key insights into her situation. Though they will not be described in detail, the dreams were all about inaction: her "sitting down, not doing anything and thinking it all through —everything—to the final end," which drove her crazy. In so doing she was using her thoughts for masturbation while fantasizing that she had to be the one to "think for everyone." Her feeling that she lacked her own identity covered up for an omnipotent fantasy in which she was everyone.

Her every effort was bent toward not seeing reality, not seeing who she herself was, not seeing others. In one dream the analyst appeared as a teacher who wanted to clean the windowpanes in her house, an idea to which she was desperately opposed. Around that time she lost her address book with "everyone's" phone number. Her dreams frequently contained scenarios that suggested her desire to remain inside the analyst.

Her desires fluctuated. On the one hand she needed to remain unborn, "not to go outside"—which she identified with her sister, who had remained inside the mother. On the other hand she repeatedly used dissociative mechanisms and projective identification to project herself onto many objects. If she went outside, she was already "in pieces": every change had the effect of emptying her further.

In order not to lose herself completely in these objects she made obsessive attempts to control her dissociation, labeling each one and assigning it a role. She even tried to keep one personality aspect with which she could define herself: "The only thing I recognize as mine are my fights." It was the only role she accepted, the fighting side of her, a partial aspect of her identity.

She began to query others as to how they saw her; she tried to get her husband to talk to her about herself. This was a desperate attempt to know about the parts she had projected onto others, to find out what her role vis-à-vis her husband was.

She set out to search for the dispersed parts of herself and started to talk about them. But she felt she could not contain them all. She could not reintroject these aspects of herself even if they were loving aspects because they were unknown to her and she was afraid they would all get mixed up inside her. Subsequent material suggested that she feared these aspects because she supposed they were stolen and did not really belong to her.

"Ricardo said something that completely threw me; he said I was passionate. I was very surprised and asked him when, and he said, 'All the time, after the beginning.' I don't understand. A girlfriend told me I was affectionate. I'm moved when I hear these things and then I feel like I play a part in what happens around me. But I also feel angry, because if he knew, why didn't he tell me before?"

She resented the passionate and tender parts of herself because they had been missing for so long and had become strangers to her. She also resented the objects that recognized these parts of herself, for in her mind it was as if they were robbing her.

Some aspects were more easily introjected than others. She admitted to being quicker to tenderness than to passion, thus setting up a competition among the projected parts of herself that sought reacceptance.

The state of her identity during this period can be seen in what the patient and her analyst came to call the dream of the mirrors.

Dream of the Mirrors

Marisa recounted her dream of the mirrors as follows:

I was going with a man to a hotel, by myself, I don't know, and it was a shady hotel, for couples, rented out by the hour, like the one around the corner from your house. Behind the little window at the entrance, the concierge looked everyone over and sized them up. Some respectable people were there too, and strange couples; one was a professor, my aunt and uncle, people from my family. . . . The concierge asked me if I thought the hotel was rough and I told him I didn't, but I thought it was for couples. I wanted them to see I was a decent person. Then I went back to the hotel with some girlfriends. Where the little window had been there were mirrors now and you could see yourself, and in between the mirrors you could see a row of women, like telephone operators. In the mirror my hair was short, the way it was a few months ago; it suited me better. I think I'll have it cut again.

This was an important dream at the time. Here we will discuss only those parts of the dream related to the patient's efforts to get acquainted with and integrate the different parts of her personality (related to spatial, temporal, and social integration).

The hotel was the analysis itself, where every hour there is a new analyst-patient couple. The various couples were composed of the pairs she formed with the analyst in the guise of her different roles. She felt that at every session the analyst looked her over to "size up" the role she was playing and the way she interacted with the analyst in that role. She projected onto the analyst the scrutinizing glance of her own curiosity and her need to control.

One of the most significant things about this dream was the patient's attempt to distinguish the introjected figures from each other in order to know the different aspects of her identity, the "respectable" figures and the "strange" ones, the unaccepted and unknown.

We became aware that the two parts of the dream represented two stages of her analysis. During the first stage, when she arrived at the hotel/place of analysis, she did not know if she was alone or together with her masculine side, the part that, as seen earlier, was wound up in her omnipotent bun-penis-nipple image.

During the second stage, when she returned to the same window where the concierge (from whom she had to hide the truth) had been scrutinizing her, she found instead mirrors in which to see herself. The breast-mirror returns her image, does not devour her like the transparent breast.

But the mirror is still fragmented; there are numerous mirrors. The patient is herself and many girlfriends; the analyst is many telephone operators. But the operators are in between the mirrors, trying to communicate with one another. This image represented her need to have the analyst reflect every part of herself as well as her need to integrate the different aspects of herself.

A haircut for Marisa meant accepting the loss of the omnipotent fantasy to "be" the couple and seeing herself more attractively as a woman. This in turn implied recognizing the existence of the opposite sex and her need for it—a realization one normally develops in adolescence.

In the following fragment we see another example of how difficult it was for Marisa to recognize her achievements: "Monday was funny, because my back teeth hurt; I thought they were infected but I didn't tell you, instead I talked about going to see a doctor about stomach massages and to get those pills. And you interpreted my sexual relations as food, and I didn't say a word; I don't know why, I didn't put it together, as if it had nothing to do with any of it. Then I went to the dentist and what happened is I have a wisdom tooth coming in."

She hid this growth from the analyst, satisfying her own fantasy of being ill. She said nothing about it because she believed that growing would separate her from the analyst; being ill united her with the analyst, just as it had with her mother. It seemed that to be accepted she had to be the toothless child who had no wisdom of her own.

This material illustrates that her difficulty in recognizing the achievements and possessions that belong to her goes hand in hand with her difficulty in taking on new roles. Assuming new roles implied losing her connection to her mother. This idea resided in her fantasy that achievements, growth, or new roles —which would consolidate her identity—meant wisdom teeth, with which she could gnash her mother to pieces and never get her back.

Because of her problem in receiving and containing different parts of herself, and because of the fear the parts of herself aroused, Marisa was in effect asking the analyst to gather the parts of herself and look after them. This was her way, one of many, of expressing her fear of disintegration after separating from analysis, and it corresponded to the fantasy that she must have felt as a baby: that her mother would open the enveloping arms and drop her, smashing her to pieces.

The month before Marisa's scheduled departure, her husband made his traveling plans; but Marisa decided—after much agonizing—to remain behind until she had completed her degree requirements. Her decision was important in more than one sense: first, deciding when to leave meant she accepted the idea of leaving; that is, she was accepting the part of her identity that was part of a couple. Second, by deciding to leave after graduation she was deciding how to leave. She was recognizing another part of her identity as a person with her own interests, as a professional.

After Ricardo left, she was on her own. Rather than rely on her father's connections she found a notary from among *her* friends to take care of final business matters. She was greatly surprised to discover that she had never bothered to find out whose name was on the lease of her apartment. She even managed to resolve some matters which her husband had left in the hands of irresponsible people.

Finally Marisa passed her last exam and graduated. She came to her session one day with a radiant face and said, "I graduated. I was going to call you but I didn't. I thought it was just another formality." It was pointed out to her that there was a discrepancy between the words she was saying and her tone of voice and facial expression.

"Papa came to wait for me after the exam, which I hadn't expected. At first he was very happy but then right away he started to ruin it. He said if I was smart I wouldn't go near another book. I asked if I could phone Ricardo to tell him the news and Papa started getting nervous. Afterwards my uncle came and said there was some problem and they had to make a large payment. Papa acted as if someone had died."

The interpretation here was that she was jealous of her father's money—omnipotent feces that were more valuable to her father than the ones she herself could produce. She believed that her graduation had caused her father to lose the money he valued so highly, or that she had killed someone valuable.

"The thing is, I also wanted to talk to the assistant who had helped me prepare for the exam but since Papa was there I didn't get to do it."

The part of herself that submits to her father and feels guilty toward him had not permitted her to communicate with the part of herself that prized her graduation or with the person who had helped her achieve her goal. Similarly, she could not communicate her happiness to her analyst; she would only be complying with a formality. Her mother, who did not appear in any of this, was not contacted either: "I don't know why I didn't include Mama. She even called me yesterday to tell me that she found out third-hand that things are going very well for Papa; he hadn't breathed a word to her. After all the hard times she's put up with, when he begins to do well, he doesn't tell her."

The analyst was not included either; just as Papa had not told Mama, Marisa did not tell her analyst that things were going well for her: she was afraid the analyst would be angry because now that the analysis was yielding results, the patient was going away.

"The truth is, Mama has changed a lot. Before, she used to make fun of me, telling me that the only career I would have was to be a mother, but later on she helped a lot with the baby so I could study. Without her I couldn't have graduated.

"Yesterday I was sorry I couldn't call my assistant or thank Mama or call you. I realize I'm including you among the people who care the most about my graduation. But something strange happens, I can't express my gratitude because if I do it ceases to be 'mine'" (as if she still feared being emptied again).

This was Marisa's way of saying that her image of her analyst had changed a lot, that she thinks the analyst helped her study and finish her education, but that she needs the analyst to accept and understand the fact that she can not thank her, although implicit in her acknowledgment of the impossibility is her desire to please. This was the best she could offer the analyst in place of thanks.

The fact that her image of the analyst as mother had changed was what prevented her from having to flatly deny her achievements. Still, her persecutory and depressive anxieties had not ebbed sufficiently for her to be able to express thanks without feeling that she thereby would lose possession of her achievements.

Marisa's final sessions were spent talking about fantasies, future plans, and her anxiety over the separation: "It's incredible; I was told I could get a work visa instead of a family visa, and that's what I did. Where it says "profession," I wrote in my profession for the first time. It was thrilling! Now that I've graduated I have more desire to work, to do something and not always be just a student. But that desire comes and goes. Sometimes I think my separation from you is terrifying and I feel bad that I didn't get more from analysis; and other times I think I got a good deal out of it and the separation doesn't seem so terrible."

Synthesis

Migration, as we have said, comprises multiple traumas and involves numerous changes of external reality, with all the subsequent repercussions on a person's inner reality. A securely established bond with a good "inner" object gives the ego the ability to endure and work through both the internal and external changes and to become personally enriched by them.

As we have seen, this was not the case with Marisa. Her childhood history revealed that she was exposed to traumatic changes and had a relationship with highly unstable objects in which she could not easily place her trust.

The familiar refrain "Every time we say goodbye I die a little" took on more dramatic overtones for Marisa when she said, "It's like being at your own funeral; everyone is talking about the future and making plans in which you are no longer included." And when she discussed the "other country" she said, "No one will know me; I'll be a nobody there."

The feeling of "being nobody" reactivated the feelings she had experienced at her mother's breast. Migration thrust upon Marisa a new birth, which she unconsciously equated with death and ceasing to exist. In the other country she would be nobody, she would again find herself at a breast which ignored her. Her birth fantasy was charged with all the life experiences related to her late weaning and the forbidden use of her teeth, the delay in changing to solids in the early genital phase resulting in her fantasies of tearing the breast, the penis, and the mother's insides in frustration. In other words, birth to her was an emptying of her contents, the unconscious fantasy behind the fear of losing one's identity.

The emptiness fantasy had a variety of sources: (1) fantasies of parts of herself spilling out (projective identification in separation situations: birth, weaning, voyages); (2) difficulty in reintrojecting these parts of herself because she considered it a dangerous task and doubted that the breast could reduce the danger; (3) later introjection and projective identification with a breast that is drained to the point of exhaustion; (4) hostile fantasies, mobilized by envy and jealousy of the early Oedipal phase, causing activation of the same mechanisms on the image of the emptied mother; (5) fantasies, confirmed by actual traumatic events, of having been vengefully emptied by the mother; (6) fantasies in sexual relations that the penis would empty her.

All these account for the fantasy of catastrophic birth which determined the extremely persecutory nature of her migration experience.

Whether leaving one's native country will acquire the characteristics of a depressive birth depends on what has enabled the individual to feel rich and full throughout his development. One feels rich and full when one has enough inner possessions, acquired through introjective identifications; a stable, secure inner object and therefore a firmly established sense of identity. Then one can cope with the tremendous losses that migration presupposes. Migration always contains the risk of a catastrophic birth.

6

THE DILEMMA

TO LEAVE OR NOT TO LEAVE?

What fuels a person's desire to leave his country?

The desire to leave can well up as something that surprises even the person who feels it, like a thought that wafts in the wind without ever entering one's mind; at a particular time, one does not know why exactly, one becomes receptive to the idea, lets it in. In other cases the idea of leaving responds to a long-harbored desire, considered impossible to launch, perhaps previously satisfied only in fantasy.

There may be external reasons which justify or sustain the desire. For example, one's reason for moving to new surroundings may be to seek opportunities for economic betterment for oneself or one's children, as occurs when families leave small towns to move to cities. Some may be encouraged to leave by work or study opportunities in other countries where one stands a better chance of developing or perfecting certain skills and thus of achieving one's goal.

Yet, real though these reasons may be, at a deeper level they may be used as rationalizations so that other, inner needs (conflictive or not) may be satisfied. A person may seek new horizons, new experiences, other cultures and philosophies of life in his thirst for knowledge and desire to discover things distant and unknown (possibly forbidden or idealized, along the lines set out in chapter 1). In some situations, the desire to leave may come from an attempt to escape persecution. In these cases, rather than *heading toward* the unknown because of the good or betterment one believes it has to offer, departure is a matter of *escaping from* the known place and its bad or persecutory experiences.

The desire to leave is not always acted upon. Not only may there be external obstacles in the way of emigration, but the desire to leave may be in conflict with the tendency to hang onto the safe and familiar, a tendency that all individuals have to a greater or lesser degree. Philobatic and ocnophilic attitudes, mentioned previously, are present in different proportions in all people and cause conflicts of ambivalence, brought into bold relief by the person's desire to leave a familiar place.

If a person's predominant reaction to change is distress, anxiety may be produced by his inner conflicts but also be linked to his relationship to the outer world. Generally, a person has the sensation that something in him remains constant no matter what changes are taking place around him. Nevertheless there are some circumstances in which the subject cannot tolerate the changes occurring in his everyday reality. When this happens, his feelings about the outside world and, simultaneously, about his own identity (the self) are thrown into disarray.

One consequence of the resulting confusion may be anxiety in the face of change, which in turn creates a need to reassure oneself that nothing has changed, that everything remains as it was. When in the throes of anxiety, some individuals do their best to avoid moving to a place where new realities reign, since change inevitably implies an incursion into the unknown, a decision to take on an unpredictable future, come what may. Anxiety leads inexorably to feelings of anguish and depression, a need to stick fast to what is familiar, and a need to resort to all kinds of justification in order to avoid change.

The individual is confronted with the primary fears of losing established structures and of losing familiarity with prescribed rules of social behavior. In the wake of such fears a person experiences deep feelings of insecurity, increased isolation, loneliness, and a fundamentally weakened sense of belonging to an established social group. Even people who feel able to tolerate the changes that are part and parcel of migration and who have valid inner or external reasons for leaving their homelands must go through a difficult developmental process, including the inevitable wavering until they make the final decision to leave.

During this process the person in charge of the family group has to take responsibility for making a decision which also affects those closest to him. Those who are dependent on him may feel admiration and gratitude toward him for making such a decision, which may correspond to their own unspoken desires: thus the decision-maker becomes the repository and executor of the family group's fantasies.

Should any setback or disappointment occur along the way, however, the decision-maker will be faced with reproach and complaints from those traveling with him. Latent or overt hostility will sometimes be directed toward him by his dependents, for his decision affects their life plans and shapes their past, present, and future.

The dependents may experience depression, impotence, resentment, or the desire to take revenge. The following material is from a female adolescent whose father decided for professional reasons to emigrate with his family to another country:

> Oh, I'm so mad . . . and feel so anxious. . . . My parents decided we're leaving the country at the end of the year. I'm so mad at Papa! Everything revolves around him. The rest of us don't count! . . . Mama is always sad. She has security here. . . . And even so, she defends Papa, she says he's having a hard time, he has headaches, so we can't even say a word against it. . . . One good thing; I received a letter from N. in England. That's some consolation, like having an "investment" abroad. But this business of having to leave! I'll never forgive Papa. In two years I'll come of age and if they don't come back, I'll come on my own. They're planning to rent out our house. Can you imagine what it would be like to come back and find other people living in your house?

Having something positive abroad was small consolation for what the patient experienced as a massive loss of all her things, her house, and her place in analysis, which would be "rented out."

"Oh . . . and the dreams I've had! . . . I was with D., S., and J. [friends]. They were talking, and I said, 'Do you realize I'm going away?' And they paid no attention, they said Yes and kept right on talking." Seeing that life continued as if no one needed her, the patient felt dead in the eyes of everyone, including her analyst. She felt like a phantom who hears and sees but is not seen or heeded by others. And the thought that no one could understand the intensity of her pain drove her to despair.

The patient came to the next session with a bad cold. She related that there had been a snowstorm in the city her father was visiting at the time. Obviously, she was identifying with him, whom she perceived as the aggressor, and on whom her fate depended. *She* was having headaches and it was *she* who was exposed, so it seemed, to the cold of the faraway city (leaving aside for the moment the other meanings of the storm and cold weather). When the analyst told her this, she responded, "Oh yes, it's true. Well, I don't want to be my father, but yesterday I did something he always does and afterwards I dreamed about it. I bought raspberry jam, but since everyone in the house likes it and they finish it right away, I hid it among the vegetables so it wouldn't be so visible. And I dreamed that I went to open the refrigerator at home and my father had hidden the chocolates in boxes so they wouldn't be seen." She experienced her father as the one who deprived her of everything she would have to leave behind —analysis, mother country, childhood food, sweetness, appetizing things—keeping it all for himself.

She felt something had broken down in her communication with others: it was as if she were already in the other world. She couldn't share her feelings with anyone; she thought they were indifferent to her suffering. On the other hand, if others expressed sorrow, she blocked it: "When I come back everyone will be different. They can't turn into petrified wood, not moving or changing until I return just so that I can find everything the same." She was acknowledging here the losses that were inevitable, although she planned to return. "Friendship is made by sharing things: and here everyone will continue to share things that I'll have no part in. I'll be living over there as if 'suspended' until I come back. . . . I feel what is happening but I'm hardened. I especially notice it if I see others getting soft: my friends cry, and I'm hardened."

A person who decides to emigrate needs support to make his decision firm and to face up to the annoyance and criticism of those who remain, the friends, neighbors, relatives, and colleagues who will be left behind. Indeed, the people around him start to separate into different camps according to the attitude they adopt toward his departure plans: those who welcome, encourage, or even envy him; those who object and discredit him; and those who grow depressed and anxious.

The environment in general begins to take on different aspects in relation to his plans: The prospective emigré may denigrate the place about to be left behind, magnify its shortcomings, seek justifications for leaving, tend to exaggerate the charms of the new place. But these emotions and fantasies may quickly become inverted. This phase bears all the signs of a time in which an individual is on "the razor's edge" (Grinberg, 1978), easily and abruptly swayed by contradictory feelings.

A clinical fragment will serve as an illustration of this phenomenon. The patient in question had considered Rome the loveliest city in the world, with the bluest skies, an age-old culture, priceless artistic treasures, and kindly inhabitants. Of course, he viewed his native city as dirty, with endlessly gray skies and a pall of pollution that blocked out the sun. However, when he returned home after a short trip prior to emigrating, these feelings alternated dangerously, and he became worried:

> While I was in Rome by myself I felt terrified, intimidated, enclosed within myself: I only went out when I had to, to see the people I absolutely had to see. . . . I even wondered once before going into a coffee shop if the waiter would look at me in a nasty way. How strange! The city I was so fond of

seemed ugly and dark and its people, whom I always considered so friendly, seemed hostile. My surprise in coming back to my city was that it wasn't as dark as I'd recalled: the clean air and blue skies surprised me. . . . Our relationship to our friends has changed, and the dividing line has been drawn between those who do and those who don't accept our migration. Some people are angry because we're leaving and say we're crazy; others say it will be good for us to go but they prefer to stay where they are. It makes us wonder: if this country is good enough for them, why not for us? The only people we feel comfortable with are others who are leaving or who probably want to leave.

These two examples reflect prototypical situations: that of the individual who has no decision-making power and is "forced" to emigrate despite her opposition; and that of the decision-maker who chooses to emigrate and assumes the responsibility of making his family emigrate.

Whether or not there is a real possibility of return may substantially modify the feelings aroused at departure time, as we shall see in a later chapter: the great difference between voluntary, desired migrations and involuntary ones, between definitive, temporary migrations with fixed return dates and those that last indefinitely, lies in the possibility of returning home.

Whatever its possible permutations and nuances, leaving is painful. Sometimes the pain is veiled by the business at hand, procedural worries and contingency plans, or by the excitement and expectations attached to the voyage; at other times the pain is most acutely felt.

A female patient described her memory of her departure in this way:

Leaving was awful. Very hard. . . . Terribly painful and wrenching. I was leaving it all behind, going to meet a future. . . . Only God, if he exists, knew how it would turn out. . . . I couldn't erase from my mind the faces of my friends and family at the airport, watching us from the other side of the plate glass window, where I couldn't hear or touch them. I saw them as if they were in a photograph or a movie, but I wouldn't be able to hug them again for a long time, knowing as I did that all of our destinies were uncertain. I had to summon all my strength not to break down and cry, and even so I felt my heart bleed to leave behind my entire past, my whole life, my loved ones and my house — for years, my pride and joy — now abandoned.

When the psychic pain is not borne as depressive suffering, it may become transformed into a feeling of persecution in which the person experiences departure profoundly as an expulsion from home because of being "unloved," even though it may be undertaken on his own initiative.

Thus, a young woman who had emigrated with her husband and children complained bitterly that her parents had not fought tooth and nail to prevent her departure; she thought that they were glad she was going away. Her persecutory fantasy seemed to relate specifically to her mother and sisters, for whom her departure eliminated her as a rival and who remained close to the father.

Another way of counteracting the pain of detaching oneself is to live in a manic way, denying sorrow and feeling triumphant over those who are staying behind, judging them to be limited, inept, endangered, or impoverished. Maniacal defenses generally are called upon when to the pain of separation are joined strong guilt feelings for abandoning those who remain — sometimes including dead, endangered, or defenseless relatives.

Although we have referred to psychic pain, it would be useful to clarify that while they may experience it, some people cannot endure it, especially when the pain occurs as a result of separation and the person's previous equilibrium is upset. Bion noted (1970) that some individuals have such an intolerance for pain and frustration that they can feel neither pain nor pleasure.

The nature of the pain we are describing permits no easy definition. Although linked to feelings of loss, it is not what could be called depression nor is it, strictly speaking, anxiety, though it does include elements of anguish. People usually experience it as something nearly physical, while knowing that it is neither hypochondriacal nor psychosomatic: it is as if it lies on the border between the physical and the mental. The important distinction is that the kind of pain felt by those in the process of emigration is not analogous to the psychic pain of depression: it does not come from concern and responsibility for object loss. This pain is of a more primitive and less conscious character because it is a throwback to the more regressive mechanisms of the paranoid-schizoid phase. In other words, as Betty Joseph (1978) has said, "the experience of this pain is not quite grief, although it may contain the seeds of the ability to feel grief."

To the extent that the individual can assimilate the experience of his migration as time goes by, integrating denied and dissociated aspects and feelings, he will grow enough to be able to feel his pain—what popular parlance would refer to as growing pains. He will then have a greater knowledge of the experiences he has lived through. It will not be mere intellectual knowledge (K link) but what Bion has termed the more experiential "becoming O." He will not only "know" that he is emigrating, he will "be" an emigrant.

Bion (1962) uses the word *link* to describe an emotional experience in which two people, or two parts of the same person, are in a relationship to each other. Certain basic emotions are always present when there is a link. Bion suggests that three of these emotions, L-love, H-hate, and K-knowledge, are the most important emotions possible in the relationship between two objects. The K, or knowledge, link corresponds to a subject that seeks to know an object and an object that lends itself to being known. It may also represent the individual who seeks through introspection to know the truth about himself. This nuance is expressed in the painful feeling behind the question, How can X [the subject] know anything? One must distinguish the acquisition of knowledge, which comes about as a result of modification of pain (then the knowledge obtained will be used for new discoveries), from possession of knowledge, which is used to avoid painful experiences, as occurs with persons in whom maniacal defenses and omnipotence predominate, and with those for whom true learning from emotional experience is impossible. Avoidance of pain may be at the service of the activity called "minus K link"—unknowing, in which denial, envy, and voracity predominate: in such situations no discovery, learning, or development is possible.

Bion (1970) notes that "transformations into O" are those that effectively promote change, growth, the search for truth, and the achievement of insight. "O" represents ultimate, unknowable reality, infinity, the absolute truth contained in and inherent to any object.

This psychic reality cannot be known; one can only have "been." Bion calls this "becoming O." It means going beyond knowing about reality. The transformation into O is like "being what one is" or "embodying one's own truth." For this very reason such transformation is feared and resisted.

To be an emigrant, then, is very different from "knowing" that one is emigrating. "Being" implies assuming fully and deeply the absolute responsibilities that go with being an emigrant. To achieve this, one must inhabit mental and emotional states that are not easy to endure. Thus people need to resort to various defensive devices in order to limit themselves to knowing they are, without being, emigrants.

7

THOSE LEFT BEHIND

The reactions of those who remain behind when others emigrate, and the nature of their feelings, depend upon the quality and intensity of the bonds that unite them with those who are leaving. Inevitably there is a sense of loss and abandonment when close relatives separate. Those who remain feel overcome by sorrow and depressive feelings and are not free of hostility toward the departing person for the suffering he is causing. Sometimes, if circumstances preclude a rapid return or the trip from the first is planned as definitive, the separation is experienced as a death.

The one who leaves dies, and so does the one who stays behind. The feelings of mourning with which each side responds to the separation may be compared to those one has at the death of a loved one. The unconscious association between leaving and dying can be extremely intense, as we saw earlier in the case of the teenage girl who felt that by leaving she died in the eyes of others. In another case, a teenage girl stayed behind while her brother emigrated far away, planning never to return. She cried for several days after his departure and then was amazed when she received his first letter: in her desperation she had thought that any communication with him was out of the question, as if he had truly traveled to "another world."

The concept of mourning implies a complex, dynamic process involving the entire personality and including all the functions, conscious or unconscious, of the ego, its attitudes, defenses, and in particular its relation to others.

Etymologically, the Spanish word for "mourning" (*duelo*) derives from the word for pain and duel, or a two-sided challenge or combat. Both meanings can be applied to the suffering caused by the losses of objects and those parts of the self that are projected onto objects. Both senses of the word apply to the tremendous psychic strength it takes to regain one's connection to reality and to the combat being waged in order to rid oneself of the persecutory aspects of the lost object and assimilate its positive, kind aspects. The two meanings of the term are particularly applicable to emigrants. They feel pain for what they are leaving behind and also must confront challenges in the new place.

Feelings of pain and guilt over the loss of parts of the self (feelings previously projected onto the object) normally either aggravate or disturb the mourning process (Grinberg, 1963). We think that the difference between the normal development of mourning and its pathological variation can be traced to two types of guilt: persecutory and depressive. Persecutory guilt is at the root of pathological mourning, which frequently presents somatizations or results in symptoms of melancholy or other forms of psychosis. Depressive guilt, on the other hand, manifests itself through worry, sorrow, and an authentic reparatory tendency which enables the person to pass through the mourning process more effectively.

The parents of an emigrating child, for example, may experience the loss of the child as if by death and may also fear that their own deaths are near, that they will never see their child again. These situations can be pathetic and wrenching for the mixture of depressive and persecutory anxieties inherent in them. In fantasy the parents blame the child for bringing them to grief, for depriving them of parental expectations and future gratifications, and for robbing them of years of their lives. Of course these feelings are reversed if the child is compelled to emigrate by political or ideological circumstances, for example, and must leave suddenly to avoid imprisonment or save his life. Then the sorrow of the departure is amply compensated by the relief the parents feel at knowing that the child will be safe from persecution and danger. However, under different circumstances, the parents can feel so ambivalent about the departure that generational conflicts or hostility from other sources prevail.

The emigrant's peer group passes through a host of emotional states covering the entire spectrum, depending on the reasons for the emigrant's departure and the environmental conditions and context for those remaining behind as well as the affective links between the parties.

A patient once related the comment one of his best friends had made upon learning of his decision to go abroad for a few years. (The patient had won a scholarship for professional advancement.) The friend had grown pale and in a voice trembling with feeling and anguish had exclaimed, "What a void [this will leave in my life]!" The image of a void synthesized the feelings of loss and emptiness which had engulfed the friend upon hearing the unexpected news. The same patient remarked that in contrast other colleagues, upon learning of his plans, reacted with overt or disguised envy and hostility. One of them said outright, "I'd leave too if I could."

Frequently the departing person becomes the repository of his peer group's projected fantasies. The context of these fantasies may reflect others' desires to emigrate, a desire they try to satisfy via projective identification with the person actually carrying them out. Often the comment is, "It's a good thing one of us can leave" or "We'll all reap the benefits." Occasionally, the departing person may feel like a scapegoat for everything that is undesirable or feared: he carries around others' guilt, expiating it through losing everything by leaving. Those who remain behind, however, are freed and can continue to enjoy what they possess.

Those who remain may also feel a sense of satisfaction from getting rid of a rival with whom they were in strong competition and whose departure leaves them with an open field.

Just as the departing person uses defense mechanisms to counteract the pain of leaving, so too do those who are left behind. They may attempt to negate or underestimate the momentousness of the separation; they will say things like "We'll be in touch," "We'll see each other soon," "We'll write often," "In the jet age, no distance is too far," and so forth.

The defenses may also be paranoid: those left behind may feel betrayed by those who are leaving and thus may react angrily or with annoyance, accusing the departing person of flippancy or a lack of responsibility and consideration toward those who had shared many vital experiences with him.

And we must not overlook a possible melancholic reaction, characterized by self-reproach, attributing to oneself either direct or indirect responsibility for losing the person who is leaving. Melancholic identification with the person who is far away is similar to the melancholic identification which occurs during the mourning process in the case of someone whom one has loved ambivalently.

Hypochondriacal symptoms and somatizations which appear shortly after a significant person's departure (for example, a father who suffers a heart attack after his son leaves) may be a defensive means of maintaining control of the absent object.

It may be inferred from the above that the decision to leave or emigrate is not an isolated fact or of exclusive concern to the person who makes the decision. As we have seen, there is a series of consequences to the individual's environment as well as to him.

Migration, in our view, constitutes a *catastrophic change* insofar as certain structures are exchanged for others and the changes entail periods of disorganization, pain, and frustration. These vicissitudes, if worked through and overcome, provide the possibility of true growth and development of the personality. But sometimes the migratory experience ends in catastrophe not only for the emigrant but also for some of those he left behind.

We know that among those who remain behind there are some who, by virtue of their especially close relationship with the person who emigrates, belong in a separate category: for example, children who do not emigrate together with their parents. The children may remain temporarily (although possibly for a period of years) with close friends or relatives in the country of origin while awaiting their parents' eventual return.

This occurs rather frequently in countries with high rates of emigration, such as Spain. In the past, parents, motivated by poverty, would leave to "do America," as the popular expression went, hoping to return as "Indianos" after making their fortunes. Many of the unsuccessful did not return at all to avoid facing the fact that their dreams had shattered. In recent decades this kind of migration is taking place in the direction of the more developed European countries such as Germany and Switzerland.

Children left behind by their parents may develop symptoms that are clearly connected to their predicament. Some children develop symptoms shortly after the parents' departure; others develop them as a reaction to the parents' return. Though seemingly paradoxical, such behavior is reminiscent of children who hurt themselves in their parents' absence and cry or complain when the parents return: it is the child's way of accusing and reproaching the parent. By acting this way the child also attempts to be seen again as an object by the person toward whom the crying is directed.

Such was the case with Javier, whose parents (Spaniards) were working in Germany when his mother became pregnant with him. He was an unwanted child, and his birth seriously interfered with his parents' plans. The mother returned to Spain only to give birth and then left the child in the care of his grandparents.

Two years later, as a result of a second pregnancy, from which a daughter was born, the parents decided to return to Spain. It was then that Javier was reincorporated into their lives. But he did not really become part of the family. His resentment over being abandoned and his envy toward his sister, who was not abandoned, were manifested in a variety of ways. He harassed his mother relentlessly with complaints of abdominal pains, vomiting, angina, and pain in one leg—pains which subsided when treated with ordinary analgesics and even placebos. After his parents' return, Javier had frequent nightmares; he dreamed that Dracula or a wolf man was about to bite him and also that he was a policeman who killed robbers.

His symptoms showed that the frustration and lack of affection he had suffered by being left behind had made him internalize his parents as persecutory and harmful objects that were attacking his insides, producing pain and emptiness. In addition, he felt that during his early years he had been robbed of direct care and parental support, to which he felt he was entitled. His parents had not been helpers or witnesses of his early achievements (eating, talking, walking). Javier's resentment and revenge fantasies then attacked his achievements when his parents returned; for this reason he had eating problems (stomach pains, vomiting, weight loss), locomotion problems (pain in his leg), and school problems (talking, learning). In his nightmares not only was he a policeman defending himself against thieves and the wolf man and Dracula, who wanted to bite him, but at another level, by means of his projections, these characters represented his own voracious desires and increased oral sadism, all resulting from his frustration.

At the age of seven, after five years of inconclusive physical examinations, Javier was sent by his pediatrician for psychological testing.

Javier's drawings representing his family speak volumes: he drew a multitude of relatives—grandparents, aunts and uncles, cousins, grandmothers with large breasts, his sister playing with cups, and himself playing with a ball—but he drew himself as the youngest in the family. He forgot altogether to draw his parents; he added them later, drawn small and in a corner, "busy working." In some drawings he included a dog which, he said, "is dead now but he's the one who always defended me."

He commented that the family drawing "didn't come out right," that "the father came out crooked," that he "had a lot more relatives but they don't fit." In other drawings the parents appeared as faceless figures; only when Javier included himself as a small child clinging to his mother did he add features to his parents' faces.

Perhaps of greatest significance was the way Javier repeatedly represented himself and his sister: he was always playing with a ball, but with one leg separated from his body. Just as he was "the member" separated from the family unit, he was the "dismembered" one of the group. His sister was playing

"Mommy" with a doll, but the doll rather leans on the sister's thorax while the sister's arms are at her sides, not holding the baby—just as Javier was not held by his mother. Her indifferent attitude and lack of support were striking.

The drawings point up Javier's use of manic defenses as an effort to compensate for the absence of his parents: he substitutes a multitude of other relatives for them. The two grandmothers who raised him have large breasts, in contrast to the little cup-breasts of the sister, who was raised by the mother. It is understandable that he would forget at first to include his parents in the drawing, just as they "forgot" to take him with them. And when he did draw the parents he reduced them in size so as to devalue them, denying their importance in his life.

His parents for a long time were faceless people to him; they took on definite features only when he included himself in the scene as a small child able to hold onto his mother.

When he comments that his family "didn't come out right" in the drawing or that his father "came out crooked," he is saying in an affecting way that he feels his parents did not fulfill their proper functions toward him.

His reference to the dog "who died but was always the one who defended me" may be an allusion to an aspect of himself: his capacity for self-defense was extinguished (died) because of parental neglect. This experience appears again in the drawing of the separated member (the leg that hurt him), which was interpreted as his feeling of being dismembered from the family. This feeling is seen again pathetically in the image of his sister, who is playing "Mommy" with a doll that is only superficially "attached" to her and not at all "supported."

8

ARRIVAL IN THE

NEW LAND

An emigrant's voyage aboard a tempest-tossed ship making its way slowly to a new world has been compared to the stormy and agitated period of adolescence, the long voyage from childhood to adulthood. The emigrants on board, having left behind the world they know, move toward a world of which they do not yet have a realistic picture. Far from the shore, they live in an unreal state shared only with their shipboard companions. As the word *shipmates* denotes, these travel companions become a new family to the emigrant. The deep resonance of the word has not lost currency even now that one can emigrate by plane as well as by boat.

Emigrants traveling by boat or plane toward a world still unreal to them do not know until they have lived it that much time will elapse, even after they have touched terra firma, before they feel that the ground beneath them is truly firm. The "seasickness" of their trip does not easily vanish on land. Migration is such a long process that perhaps it never really ends, just as the emigrant may never lose the accent of his native language.

A female patient discovered only after years of analysis how painful the migration that she took on lightly and happily as a young girl had actually been. "If I had realized how painful it all was I wouldn't have been able to make it; I would have collapsed."

During this patient's analysis, the purchase of furniture enabled her to discover one meaning of her migration that had previously escaped her. Until then, apparently for financial reasons as well as style preferences, she had decorated her home in the new land with a profusion of pillows, fabric, cushions on the floor, rugs on the walls, and so on. Her description of her home put one in mind of a bedouin tent richly adorned and lavishly covered with rugs, made of easily transportable elements to match a nomad or gypsy life-style.

Her migratory experience had transformed her into an insecure little girl who felt that she had been abandoned and that everything had suddenly become temporary. There was no guarantee that she would stay in one place, and for that reason everything had to be transportable in case she had to move again. The pillows and cushions were the soft, fluffy, warm breasts with which she needed to surround herself to offset the feeling of being a defenseless orphan. Only much later in her life, when through analysis she found more stable support in her inner and outer surroundings, was she able to buy strong, solid furniture—beds and chairs—to hold her more firmly; for her they represented the prospect of durability.

The insecure feelings that newly arrived immigrants experience arise not only from uncertainty and anxiety in the face of the unknown but also from the inevitable regression that goes hand in hand with these anxieties. It is the regression which makes the immigrant feel defenseless and inhibited at times, incapable of making effective use of the resources he possesses, which constitutes his true "baggage." This situation is presented movingly and eloquently in Kafka's novel *Amerika* as he describes the emotion assailing his young protagonist, Karl, when the boat on which he is traveling enters New York harbor and Karl prepares to disembark, his box hoisted on his shoulder: "A sudden burst of sunshine seemed to illumine the Statue of Liberty, so that he saw it in a new light, although he had sighted it long before." But his euphoria turns to discomfort when moments later his box disappears. In the hubbub and confusion of the landing he forgets his umbrella; when he goes below deck to retrieve it, he leaves his box for a moment at a stranger's side. "Again his thoughts turned back to the box, and he simply could not understand why he should have watched it during the voyage so vigilantly that he had almost lost his sleep over it, only to let that same box be filched from him so easily now."*

A similar experience was related by a young patient. She arrived in the new country, where she planned to do professional work, and immediately left in the trunk of a taxi her most valuable possession, the diploma which accredited her in her field. She managed to recover it some days later.

In these situations, the individual has an overriding need for someone, a person or group in the new environment, to take on the maternal and containment functions that will enable him to reorganize and survive. The stranger who steals Kafka's character's trunk represents all that is unknown to the person who is newly arrived, whatever disorganizes and confuses him and makes him schizophrenic. What he needs, then, is a familiar someone, or someone he will soon get to know in the new country.

In *Diario de un emigrante* (Diary of an Emigrant), a literary landmark in contemporary Spanish stylistics, Miguel Delibes portrays the intense, overwhelming experience of the new and unknown facing his protagonist, Lorenzo, who emigrates from Spain to Chile:

> We docked in Buenos Aires and from there took the train to Santiago. . . . By that time I was a little stunned and it occurred to me, seeing more people thronging in those streets than I had ever seen before, that five million people could walk past my nose and I wouldn't find one familiar face; and then it occurred to me that this was worse than being in the desert, and I had a feeling, like being sad about everything, and I couldn't stop. I started to remember my house, the block, and the cluster of buildings, and I said to Anita, I wonder what the old folks are doing right now, and what time it is over there.

*Franz Kafka, *Amerika*, trans. Edwin Muir (New York, New Directions, 1946), pp. 3, 9.

Earlier in the novel there had been an allusion to what we would call the perception of regression, which grows stronger as the characters approach their destination. During the crossing they had had to adjust their watches to the proper time zone. Just prior to their arrival, Lorenzo comments, "We set our watches back another half hour; and I was thinking that at this rate, soon I'd be back to wearing knickers."

The immigrant's need for a trustworthy person who can take over or neutralize the anxieties and fears he feels toward the new and unknown world can be compared to that of a child who is left alone and desperately searches for the familiar face of his mother or a mother-substitute. One model that comes close to this idea is the ethologists' notion of "imprinting," which explains the tendency of all newborns to pick out a potential provider of contact and protection. Indeed, they seem to latch on to the first one they meet, even if it belongs to another species, so long as it is available to satisfy those needs.

In 1960, Bowlby used this ethological model as the basis for developing his own theory of attachment, which studies the bond between the child and the trustworthy figures who lessen the anxiety of separation. The theory of object relations holds that such a figure is always a representative of an internal mother with protective traits who, in offering contact and containment, calms the child's anxieties.

In this connection, in order for good internal objects which have been temporarily inhibited by separation anxiety and the impact of new, unknown situations to be reactivated in a protective role, the immigrant needs to find in the external world other persons who represent "godfathers" or substitute fathers.

A newly arrived immigrant, like a newborn baby, is exceedingly sensitive. The need to feel welcome is such that any arrangement that works out or person who shows any interest whatsoever and is cordial and sympathetic makes the immigrant feel loved. In the same way, any setback can make him feel rejected by his new surroundings.

Naturally, the immigrant's first impressions have a great impact.

His reactions will have some persecutory content, depending on the nature of his object relations in the past. His objects have been internalized and will condition the paranoid intensity of his responses to the inevitable frustrations he finds along the way. If his internal object bonds are predominantly conflictive in nature, he will most probably undergo serious regression, causing him to rely on primitive defense mechanisms of the paranoid-schizoid type: more accentuated dissociations, flat denials, unpleasant situations, compensatory idealizations of partial aspects of himself, frequent and widespread use of projective identification, and so on.

The purpose of dissociation is to counteract persecutory as well as depressive anxieties and to keep at arm's length the threat of confusion which comes about because there is no clear differentiation yet between the old and the new.

At first a person's most obvious tendency is to idealize the new country, magnifying its positive qualities, and to undervalue the old country. Idealization of this sort leads to hypomanic states and usually a fleeting or temporary feeling of psychic or physical well-being. Thus, for example, some patients say they have "never felt better and haven't slept so contentedly in years." The restful sleep may be a defense against, a haven from, the experience of unpleasant, difficult circumstances. Sometimes prolonged sleep reflects depression and expresses a deep-seated fantasy to flee life. Sometimes the defense mechanism fails, and the same unconscious fantasies find expression in exactly the opposite direction, causing sleep problems such as insomnia or agitated dreams of persecution.

One must bear in mind that the new arrival must incorporate new communication codes, which are for all intents and purposes unknown or poorly grasped at first, increasing the ambiguity and contradictions contained in the information he receives (Achard and Galeano, 1982). As a result, the immigrant may feel "invaded" by what are for him "chaotic messages" or may feel "eaten up" by an unfamiliar and hostile world.

In regression to more primitive levels of mental functioning, emotions tend to be expressed in relation to primal things such as food. Food takes on special relevance because it symbolizes the earliest structured link with the mother or the mother's breast. Thus the immigrant may vehemently reject the new country's local dishes and nostalgically seek out the foods of his own country.

An Argentine woman who emigrated to the United States insisted in the early phase of her migration upon eating *empanadas* (meat pies) and *churrascos* (broiled meat) to the exclusion of all other food, so as not to lose her identity. Conversely, a son of immigrants residing in Argentina systematically refused to eat meat, the main food consumed in Argentina. He limited his diet to milk and eggs, the basis of his meals in the past, and moreover insisted that these products be imported from his native country. Clearly, he was rejecting the breast that he considered bad, unknown, and persecutory (meat) while desiring the known and idealized breast (milk and eggs from his homeland).

The immigrant may also take refuge in food to ease his anxiety, thus recreating an idealized breast that is generous and inexhaustible, with which he tries to compensate for the many losses incurred during the move. He usually eats those meals in the presence of conationals—they constitute a type of memory rite. In other cases, the person may eat in solitude, and the eating may become a compulsive, frenetic search to recover lost objects.

In the early stage of a migration, a person's mind is more occupied with the people and places he left behind than with what confronts him in the new place. Often his thinking is permeated by homesickness and imagined reencounters with people. Gradually, as he commits himself more to his new way of life and the people around him, he begins to distance himself when recalling relatives and old friends. The lengthy and frequent letters some immigrants write or receive from the old world in the early stages of their arrival in the new world eventually slow to a trickle, becoming a sign of mutual distancing.

Human beings change, as do habits and ways of life and language—even the same language. Those who leave change as much as those who remain behind. What remains unchanged

—and this has important future influence and repercussions—is the nonhuman environment, which comes to represent a significant part of a person's sense of identity. This nonhuman environment is invested with intense emotional content and tends to persist unmodified as an object of nostalgia and symbol of belonging.

Denford (1981) refers to Searles' view that the nonhuman world is a "place of experimentation and tension release." Additionally, Denford mentions Winnicott's notion of "transitional space," which may be extended to include the nonhuman world, the place where one engages in the earliest games with objects that are "not-me" and "not-mother." For Denford, losing and being deprived of one's nonhuman environment and the specially valued objects in the old environment play a large part in the immigrant's development—as decisive as losing or being deprived of the presence of loved ones.

This would help explain why many emigrants try to take all their belongings with them, irrespective of their utility: old furniture that falls apart during the trip, clothing they no longer wear, devices that do not work. Odds and ends that are worth little but carry great emotional weight may fulfill this function, which has great significance for one's sense of identity.

One patient who emigrated felt radically different when her furniture arrived, well after her arrival. She began one session, "Ever since I got here my dreams have been completely crazy, they didn't feel like my dreams, I didn't recognize them. I had never had dreams like those. It was as if I wasn't myself. . . . But a few days ago my dreams went back to normal. I think it started happening the day my furniture arrived: I felt like I was around my things again. I was touched to see them again. Every object brought back memories of a situation, a moment, a past. I felt more myself."

9

THE NEW ENVIRONMENT

The reaction of members of the new community toward the immigrant will have diverse influences on how the new immigrant settles in and adapts. This factor has generally been recognized; what has not been commonly recognized is that the native community also feels the impact of the newcomer, for his presence modifies the group structure, can throw doubt on the community's moral, political, or scientific ground rules, and can destabilize the existing group organization. Therefore, the natives will also find it a difficult task to neutralize and incorporate the presence of a stranger in their midst. It is not only the emigrant who feels his identity endangered; in a different way the community on the receiving end may feel that its cultural identity, the purity of its language, its beliefs, and its sense of group identity are also threatened.

In this regard it will be useful to develop Bion's model (1970) of the relation between contained-container ($\male \leftrightarrow \female$). This model clearly illustrates the different dynamics that can occur in the interaction between the immigrant and the receptor group and may be equally applicable to the range of emotional reactions between the person who decides to emigrate and those who stay behind.

Originally Bion applied this model to show the various possibilities for the development of a new idea, or the individual who nourishes the idea, in relation to the establishment that receives the idea.

The dynamic interreaction between the individual and the new idea (the immigrant), on the one hand, and his environment (the country that receives him), on the other, in Bion's view, qualifies as a catastrophic change that can in differing degrees disrupt the structure and composition of the group. The immigrant, with all his baggage and personality traits, represents the "new idea-contained" (♂), which may receive diverse responses from the container-receptor group (♀). Extremes range from enthusiastic acceptance to outright rejection.

The term "catastrophic change" refers to a series of events or facts that are linked to one another by "constant conjunction." "Constant conjunction," a concept taken from Hume, refers to the fact that certain observable data regularly appear to be linked. Among these events or facts or data are violence, subversion of the system, and invariance—whatever makes one recognize aspects of the old in the new structure.

Migration constitutes a catastrophic change to the extent that certain structures become transformed into others, and in the process of change there are periods of pain, disorganization, and frustration. If these are overcome and worked through, the changes offer the possibility of true growth and enriched development of the personality.

But migration is not always a catastrophic change: it can develop into a true catastrophe. Whether it becomes one or the other depends in great part on the interaction between the contained and the container.

The contained element may, by sheer disruptive force, pose a threat of destruction to the container. An excess of rigidity or fear may drown the contained and thus stymie his development.

The third and most productive possibility is that each side will function with sufficient flexibility for the containing group to accept a nondestructive contained element, whose assimilation and development will be to their mutual benefit.

We have described some of the reactions an immigrant may have when he arrives in a new country: mania, depression, paranoia, confusion. Let us now see what occurs with the receptor group. First of all, a salient factor is whether the receptors participated in some way in the event itself, whether they actively invited the immigrant or were informed of his arrival and accepted it. If so, the reception will be positive; at least, overt hostility will not be displayed. If the newcomer bursts upon the scene without warning, this may engender an initially guarded response on the part of the receptor community, which will prepare to fend off any possible attack until the newcomer's intentions are known. This is especially the case if the new person is viewed as aggressive or a threat to the group.

Of course, the immigrant's attitude, personality, and conduct may confirm or modify the group's expectations and first impressions. His past history will determine his ability to project onto the environment his strong bonds with internal objects.

One must allow for the possibility that the immigrant's presence in some cases will increase the paranoid anxieties of the receptor group. The newcomer may be viewed persecutingly as an intruder who is trying to deprive the locals of their inalienable rights to enjoy the fruits of their labor, their possessions and property. In extreme cases, intense xenophobic reactions with marked hostility may result.

The immigrant can approach others if they show respect for the dignity and authenticity of his existence; however, if they refuse to recognize these and reject his presence, the immigrant will view the natives as his irreconcilable enemies.

In *The Castle* (1958), Kafka describes the animosity of the villagers toward the protagonist, a surveyor supposedly come to work in the castle. Even those who promise to protect him and try to help him say, "You are not from the Castle, you are not from the village, you aren't anything. Or rather, unfortunately, you are something, a stranger, a man who isn't wanted and is in everybody's way, a man who's always causing trouble."* What is noteworthy in this passage for our purposes is the way in which the natives attack the newcomer's identity: they react to someone who is not from there as if he were nothing, as if he did not exist, although they then admit that he is "something": "a stranger, a

*Franz Kafka, *The Castle*, trans. Willa and Edwin Muir (New York: Vintage, 1958), p. 62.

man who isn't wanted." The villagers' persecutory life experiences are so strong that they need to dehumanize the immigrant and reduce him to an inanimate object, denying his status as a person (they turn him from someone into "something") after trying to ignore his existence entirely. The passage continues, "Your ignorance of the local situation is so appalling that it makes my head go round to listen to you and compare your ideas and opinions with the real state of things. It's a kind of ignorance that can't be enlightened at one attempt, and perhaps never can be. . . . Never forget that you're the most ignorant person in the village, and be cautious."†

Often the abilities and powers attributed to the "invader" reinforce the natives' rivalry, jealousy, and envy fantasies. This may set in motion complex vicious circles with increased persecution on the one side and hate on the other in the mind of the immigrant, who does not find the reception he had hoped for and needs.

Hostility may be manifested in subtle ways—for example, by not making an effort to understand or communicate with the foreigner; rather, accentuating linguistic differences as if to confirm that it is impossible for the newcomer to understand his environment. Parties to conversations use language as a defense against newcomers, using local expressions or particularly refined and educated speech, both of which are inaccessible to the immigrant. On other occasions the locals may refer, in the foreigner's presence and without offering explanations, to events and people that belong to their history and tradition, from which the foreigner is of course excluded. Not infrequently, denigrating names for foreigners are used, or nicknames that stick for generations; these contain condensed envy that originated in overvaluation and disdain that serves as protection from envy.

Sometimes the receptor group reacts very positively to a newcomer who has unconsciously been cast in an omnipotent and idealized image, and "should be able to" resolve or help resolve

†Ibid., p. 63.

intricate problems afflicting the community. In these cases the newcomer is seen as a kind of Messianic leader and is treated with the utmost cordiality and kindness. He is offered all the help he needs to settle into the community. But since the newcomer can never satisfy its expectations, the receptor group may later react with disappointment and hostility, out of a feeling of having been cheated, thus creating more problems for the foreigner.

Because of socioeconomic conditions, some countries which are especially interested in attracting immigrants and are aware of the importance of meeting their needs make every effort to create positive, welcoming conditions. Israel, for example, has institutionalized the container functions by creating Immigrant Absorption Centers, where newcomers live together for a few months with others in the same situation while they learn the new language and the new codes and guidelines they will be expected to follow from people who act as "tutors." In other cases, already established people from the old country can fulfill the function of receiving and welcoming newcomers.

All things considered, it is not always easy for the newcomer to accept this help: it is painful to admit that he needs it. Some people find it intolerable to accept regression or to live through a humiliating kind of infantilization, having society grant them a moratorium before they are expected to fully function in new surroundings.

A mature man who was treated in short-term psychotherapy was suffering terribly. He had been a prestigious architect in his own country and had emigrated for family reasons. His problem with the language and his trouble in adapting to his new situation led him to accept a severely underpaid job not in keeping with his previous professional and social position or his intellectual capacity. He fell into a deep depression for which he sought counseling. When he could understand and tolerate his regressive state as a necessary moratorium until he could adjust to the change in his life, he managed to overcome the acute stage of his depressive crisis and confront his situation with a more positive inner disposition. This also enabled him to find more positive responses to his needs in the outside world and to make a more appropriate place for himself in the new society.

Finally, the interaction between the newcomer and the local group may be sufficiently balanced, without touching either extreme of persecution or idealization, as to allow both to participate in the process of getting to know one another, favoring the gradual integration of each, which then becomes more solid and secure.

10

DEVELOPMENT OF THE

MIGRATORY PROCESS

ASSIMILATION INTO THE

NEW ENVIRONMENT

The anxieties that appear in the initial stages of migration are of the persecutory, confusional, and depressive types. While anxieties must be considered a constant feature of any migratory process, they vary greatly in intensity, duration, and evolution.

Paranoid anxieties escalate into true panic when the demands the immigrant perceives as overwhelming become too intense, and he becomes unable to face loneliness, ignorance of the language, the search for work and housing, and so on. Some people, unable to meet these demands or fearing failure, suddenly decide at this stage to return home, provided that the conditions of their emigration allow them to turn back.

Disorienting anxiety arises from problems in differentiating one's feelings about two subjects of interest and conflict: the country and people one has left behind and the new environment. At times, migration sets up a triangular Oedipal situation between the two countries, as if each country symbolically represented one of the parents, in relation to whom ambivalence and conflicting loyalties reappear. The emigrant experiences this as if his parents were divorced, and he engages in fantasies of forming an alliance with one against the other.

Confusion increases when culture, language, place, points of reference, memories, and experiences become mixed up and superimposed on one another. Confused states also result from defensive attempts to stave off persecutory anxieties in the face of the unknown. For example, such states occur in mild form when the person transforms the unknown into something familiar: giving names to the streets of a new city that correspond to those of his native city; judging distances using as units of measurement the familiar and frequent routes he knew in the past; believing he sees familiar faces in crowds, and so on. These phenomena may be accentuated in countries that are similar to the emigrant's own or where the same language is spoken—because it has many similarities to home, the emigrant denies that it is really a different country. Paradoxically, fantasies seeming to facilitate a person's adjustment may backfire to reproduce persecutory fantasies in which people and things are seen in a sinister light, with things appearing to be what they are not and dead/alive qualities being reversed.

Depressive anxieties are created by experiences of great loss together with the fear of never being able to recover all that has been left behind. This requires a process of mourning, which, as we have said, is always difficult and sometimes assumes pathological characteristics, especially when the subject has no opportunity to recognize, feel, or express his loss and work it through.

Different types of anxieties can develop pathologically into truly psychotic states, as we shall see later. In paranoia and overt persecutory delusion, all one's surroundings are seen as hostile and dangerous, enmeshed in conspiracies whose object is to hurt or do harm to the subject. Disorienting psychosis may cause a person not only to lose his sense of identity but also to become disoriented in time and space, particularly with regard to the before and now, the there and here. It is the most commonly observed clinical disorder among hospitalized immigrants. Profound melancholy, on the other hand, consists of an intense feeling of ego impoverishment together with a sense of deprivation and an emptying of all one's content, belongings, and abilities.

These are extreme situations and are not intended as generalizations; however, one must recognize that migration promotes the outbreak of latent pathology in individuals who are particularly fragile and may provide a springboard for more or less serious psychic disturbances. As Garza-Guerrero has pointed out (1974), a distinction must be made between migration in its pathological development—with unresolved identity crisis, depressive ailments, and chronic social maladjustment—and in its healthy development, in which one experiences uneasiness about one's identity as a result of culture shock. As Ticho put it (1971), "Culture shock is a self-limiting crisis."

Some people react with manic overadjustment, rapidly identifying themselves with the habits and manner of functioning natural to inhabitants of the new country, trying to forget their own, in deference to a sense of realism. Others do just the opposite: they cling tenaciously to their own customs and language, socialize exclusively with other nationals, form closed groups that function as actual ghettoes.

In his novel *El jardín de al lado* (The Garden Next Door), José Donoso tells a story in which several crises intersect: the crisis of being an uprooted Latin American living in Spain, a crisis in the character's relation to his wife and to himself, and a crisis in the character's creative capacity and essential vitality. In one scene, a group of exiles is preparing the ritual *asado* (barbecue) on a Mediterranean beach while they proclaim in bitter, mocking tones, with wine in hand and *carnavalito* and *chamamé* music in the background, that one cannot take seriously any country that is "badly situated," where one can never see the sun set over the water, "the way it ought to be," the way it is in Chile. People who do not manage to become assimilated, who take refuge behind a fence that encloses their memories and distant affections, seem to be condemned to view life as something that always happens in a "garden next door"—on someone else's property into which they peer without being able to participate in the activities taking place there.

Clearly, the immigrant must give up part of his individuality, at least temporarily, in order to become integrated in the new environment. The greater the difference between the new community and the one to which he once belonged, the more he will have to give up. Inevitably, these surrenders or losses open the door to conflicting mourning processes because they work at cross-purposes with each individual's desire to be different from others — that is, to preserve one of the hallmarks of his identity. We can imagine his suffering when he must lose, albeit only partially, the valued symbols of his native group, among them, his culture and language. He may experience it as the equivalent of psychic castration.

One's own language, the mother tongue, is never as libidinally invested as when one lives in a country where a different language is spoken. All childhood experiences, memories, and feelings about early object relations are connected to language. Special meanings become embedded in it. Language is such a fundamental part of life that we will deal with it extensively in a later chapter.

Another major problem confronting the immigrant is how to find his place, his spot, in the new community and acquire anew the social position and professional status he enjoyed in his homeland. No one knows him, and feeling anonymous increases his inner insecurity. The theme of place appears frequently in immigrants' dreams, a place that the dreamer has difficulty finding.

Loneliness and isolation increase the immigrant's depression over his losses since he can no longer depend on the support of the familiar socio-family milieu in times of mourning. Yet, as Calvo says (1977), "The immigrant must make an exhausting effort to endure devastating feelings, sorrow for what he has lost, without buckling under. At the same time he must make equally intense efforts to continue responding adequately to current demands."

The following dream occurred shortly after a patient's migration and illustrates her experience with loss of objects and parts of the self. The depressive content is clear. She dreams that she is going to meet an aunt of hers (who belonged to the idealized part of the family and was connected to the reasons for her migration). On the way to meet her aunt, she leaves her bag and coat in a store, planning to stop by for them on the way back. Everything seems very easy and pleasant. But then it all turns difficult: she cannot find her aunt, there are hordes of people in the street; then she sees her aunt but she is far away and talking to other people, leaving the patient out of the conversation. Suddenly the dreamer realizes that the place where she left her things is not on the way. She hurries back for her belongings, but the stores have closed and her things have disappeared. Finally, she does not know how, she finds her purse, though her coat is still missing. She is relieved because she was carrying all her identification in her purse.

The scene of the dream had some elements of her native city and other details of her new place of residence. The idealized aunt, whom the patient was going to meet, represented the idealized country in which she had newly arrived. Along the way, during the migration, she had been leaving her belongings in different places, unconcerned. Her manic mechanisms take over, and at first she does not think the things she left behind were important; everything seems pleasant and easy. But soon frustration sets in because she does not feel welcomed by her aunt—the substitute mother/idealized country—of whom she expected so much. She feels excluded. Then the depressive feeling emerges over the loss of her belongings, which she tries to recover. She manages to save only her threatened and wavering sense of identity, and though she feels unprotected without her coat, she is relieved because knowing "who she is" keeps at bay her fear of a depressive collapse, which had surfaced in previous sessions, before this dream. (For reasons of relevance, we exclude the transference implications of the dream.) In the mourning process, people come face to face with their guilt feelings: those that are both of a persecutory and a depressive nature.

Analysis of another patient's dream highlights the fluctuation between the two types of guilt. She had this dream some time after her emigration. She is with her husband and children in a chalet that had belonged to them in their country. (She knew it had been sold when they left.) The current owners are not at home, but she and her husband have their old key. They place a table in the garden, as they used to do in the summertime, and just as they are about to eat and go swimming, the owners arrive. They consider it natural that the family is there, and they sit down to eat with them.

What was most striking to the patient about this dream was that in the middle of the garden surrounding the chalet there was a coffin resting on a sawhorse and covered with cloth, containing the corpse of her father, who had died some years before. In her dream the patient wonders if she will have to bury her father or leave him with the new owners of the house. She is surprised that they purchased the chalet with the "coffin in the garden." She vacillates between thinking that there is no reason she should make the funeral arrangements because the chalet no longer belongs to her, and thinking that she should see to the funeral because the corpse belongs to her. She does not know if she will have to rent a special car or if the coffin will fit in hers. She finally decides to take it in her car.

Through association, it became clear that the dream expressed the patient's attempts to work through the losses she experienced in emigrating. She was not prepared to admit that the chalet, filled with so much of her history and affections, no longer belonged to her. In the dream she tried to get it back, although she had to share it with the new owners. The coffin with the father's corpse in the middle of the garden indicated that her migration had reactivated her sorrow over his death, a condensation of all the other losses that were now at the center of her concerns. The persecutory guilt she felt had to do (in part) with abandoning her country and her dead father; this led her to try to deny her obligation toward the unburied (the mourning is not over) body that belonged to her. She tried to project this responsibility onto the new occupants of the chalet. Her irrational resentment of them for owning something that she had been so attached to in the past allowed her to justify foisting such responsibility on them. She expressed it by saying, "Since they are keeping the house, let them keep the dead bodies too."

Yet, despite the complexity and confusion of her feelings, she realized that it was she who had to take charge of burying "her dead," although she doubted her ability (inner space) to carry it out. The idea of hiring a "special car" with more space was an implicit plea to the analyst to help her contain the dead.

In all object losses a simultaneous loss of parts of the self accompanies the person's sorrow for the lost object. Any matter of concern to the state of one's ego automatically implies concern for one's sense of identity. Throughout a person's development there are many situations which threaten the self's integrity and expose it to painful, harmful experiences or partial losses, which in turn create depressive responses. The same defense mechanisms used by the ego to fight anxiety can sometimes attack the ego's structure and integration, contributing to its debilitation. The desire to make oneself complete by recovering the lost aspects of oneself is at the heart of working through the self-mourning process.

One patient spontaneously expressed this idea as follows: "Transitions take so much time! I'm going from careless to careful, from disorder to order, from migration to settlement. My brother is coming to visit. I don't know what to ask him to bring of the things I left at home. I don't know if all my things are still there: some were given away to my sisters or to friends. I have the sensation of having moved through life with an open suitcase, scattering things as I went. . . . Now I'd like to pick up whatever pieces I can."

There is one symptom in particular that we have observed in many immigrants who manage to adapt quickly after arrival to the modes, habits, and demands of the new place. They find work, learn the language, set up a home for their family, and even develop successful social and professional relationships, all in two or three years in an apparent state of psychic and physical balance. Paradoxically, at the point where they can enjoy the results of their hard work and achievements, they fall suddenly into a state of profound sadness and apathy which causes them to leave their jobs and break off ties with the external environment. We have termed this set of symptoms the postponed depression syndrome. It seems to occur when the manic defenses used during this period to achieve and maintain compulsory adaptation become exhausted. Occasionally, in place of postponed depression the migrants develop somatic manifestations such as miocardial arrest or gastric ulcer, frequent symptoms in the second or third year of migration.

Another commonly observed phenomenon among immigrants is what we might call money hypochondria, expressed as fear of poverty and homelessness. This symptom is closely related to migration; we have seen it in people who in their native countries had few economic worries but who in changed surroundings experience inner insecurity and instability.

At times, the price of the effort to overcome a problem at the emotional level is displacement of the conflict to the body. It is then that psychosomatic disturbances appear. These may be of a diverse nature: digestive symptoms (the person cannot "digest" the experience of migration, or the "new food"), respiratory symptoms (the new place is suffocating), circulatory symptoms (the environment and its demands produce pressure on the arteries and heart), and so on. The person may have a greater propensity to accidents, disguised suicide attempts. Instead of somatic symptoms, some immigrants display fantasies and hypochondriacal fears.

The seriousness of the disturbances set off by migration depends to a great extent on whether the migration was made alone, in a group, or in the company of spouse and family. Institutions that work with young people who have emigrated without their families usually put them together in groups, since they know from experience that it is a relief for emigrés to share their troubles, despite other tensions that may surface among group members.

Solid and stable ties to a spouse or family better enable emigrants to confront and endure the vicissitudes of change and to work through their sorrows. However, if these ties are conflictive, migration only sharpens the conflicts and can trigger marriage breakups or problems between parents and children. One of the most frequent manifestations of these conflicts is disparity in the way family members accept or reject the new country. Some adapt easily: they succeed, they make friends; others remain resentful, feel devalued, want to return home. At any rate, all migrations cause ruptures between the emigrant and his distant relatives, and, depending on the respective family structures (provided that they exist), these conflicts have varying repercussions.

Berenstein (1981) maintains that the members of a family unit are linked, without knowing it, by an unconscious structure whose central pillar is the complex relation between the conjugal couple and the maternal family. Some individuals, owing to their personal qualities, rebel in various ways against the social or family structure. If the decision to emigrate becomes part of this rebellion, runs counter to the family's desire or the interest of the family structure, it may have an effect on the eventual outcome of the migration. Such a decision, while apparently liberating, may cause the subject to become the mediator of the contradiction between the conjugal couple's family and the maternal family.

Perhaps the deep desire of the emigrant is to fulfill the paternal function of establishing a new context. His goal could be the creation of a new system, different from the maternal family's, that allows him to more fully affirm his exogamy.

He may experience migration as the equivalent of a heroic act in which he proclaims his independence; it may give him a feeling of triumph over his abandoned mother and father or even be the concretization of an orphan fantasy. In either extreme case, complications that come up in the evolution of the migration can be traced to feelings of guilt in the first case and an intense life experience of helplessness in the second.

The enormous importance of work as an organizing and stabilizing factor in psychic life cannot be overemphasized. This is especially true if the subject is skilled in his work and obtains certain satisfaction from it. In an immediate and evident way, work restores the immigrant's self-respect, allowing him to meet expenses and resume the functions of adulthood following the regressive period just after his arrival. At the same time, work makes one feel that one has a place in the new society. And, at a deeper level, work allows one to draw on one's creative capacity, with reparatory benefits to the self and its lost or abandoned objects.

In general, if the immigrant's personality traits are healthy, his motivation for emigrating rational (although there are always simultaneous irrational motives), the conditions of his trip adequate, and the new environment reasonably hospitable, he can gradually make a commitment to his new way of life. If his emotional state lets him be realistic, without reverting to negations or extreme dissociations, and if he can accept his limitations, he will be able to learn from the new experience and value the positive aspects of the new country. All the above, in turn, will make room for psychological enrichment and a real adjustment to his surroundings.

The "work of working through" a mourning process is long; it is a process that begins at the moment of loss, a process in which the ego plays a fundamental role. We have described two types of mourning, mourning for an object and mourning for lost aspects of the self: in our view, these two processes occur simultaneously. After the initial reactions of shock because of the sudden imbalance brought about by the massive loss of valued objects, the ego tries to reorganize itself by gradually working through its losses.

Working through is a dynamic process resulting from a dialectical movement between regression and progression. Indeed, there can be useful regression, described by Winnicott (1955) as that which seeks to replace the "false self" with the true self. Such regression is favored if the individual accepts this state as transitory.

To work something through, the individual's entire personality, including all the ego functions, has to make an enormous psychic effort to accept losses and recover an affective link to reality, overcoming denials and the effects of the various defensive mechanisms.

Dream work is actively involved in this process. In the early period there are recurrent "evacuative" types of dreams (Grinberg et al., 1967), as happen in cases of traumatic neurosis: the dreams serve the function of defusing anxiety and guilt. Later, the dreams take on a more developmental quality, with elements that represent memories of the past and relationships to loved objects. This leads to greater ego integration. When the working-through process follows its normal path, it leads to an increased creative capacity and synthetic functioning of the ego. If the ego works through a depression with positive results and feels reparatory and constructive impulses toward itself, it is more likely to experience and apply reparatory tendencies toward objects. In this way one can understand the simultaneous integration processes more thoroughly with respect to the complete object and the complete self. In the final analysis, it is this process of self-integration, if one successfully works through the period of mourning for oneself and for objects, that encourages the progressive reestablishment of one's sense of identity.

Little by little, and to the extent that he has worked through the sorrows of migration, the newcomer begins to feel that he is an integrated member of his new environment, and he comes to live like others with his own particularities of language, customs, and culture, at the same time maintaining a positive and stable relation to his own country with its language and culture without having to reject the old in order to accept and be accepted by the new. Integration, always slow and hard work, is the culmination of successive and complementary steps in the developmental process.

To recapitulate, the migratory process does not always follow the same trajectory, but it can be divided into various stages:

1.   In the first stage, the predominant feelings are intense pain for all that one has left behind or lost, fear of the unknown, deep-rooted loneliness, need, and helplessness. Paranoid, disorienting, and depressive anxieties may alternate with one another, leaving the person prone to periods of total disorganization.

2.   After a period of varying length, the feelings that arise are

sorrow for the lost world and nostalgia; the immigrant begins to recognize feelings that were previously dissociated or denied because they were unbearable. He is able to suffer his pain (growing pains) and make himself more accessible, slowly and progressively incorporating the elements of the new culture. Interaction between the inner and outer worlds becomes smoother.

3. In the third stage, the immigrant rediscovers the pleasures of thinking and wanting and recovers the ability to plan for the future, in relation to which the past is felt to be past, not a "lost paradise" to which he constantly yearns to return. The past does not interfere with the possibility of living fully in the present.

At this stage one might say that the mourning for one's native country has been worked through as far as possible; although perhaps it is a process that is never altogether completed. But this resolution makes it easier for the immigrant to integrate his native culture into the new one without having to renounce either one. Thus ego enrichment is promoted along with the consolidation of what one might call the remodeled sense of identity.

11

MIGRATION AND LANGUAGE

Given that language change is one of the most difficult problems facing the immigrant, language deserves a chapter of its own. Here we will generally consider the essence of language and its decisive influence on human evolution from earliest infancy through the development of the sense of identity, especially its influence on the individual's communicative links to his neighbors.

By language we mean a continuous, uniform product of signs and meanings that fulfills a real function in human speech. The characteristics of language contain a certain weltanschauung that determines the way its speakers perceive and apprehend reality. In creating our image of reality, language molds that reality.

Schaff (1969) considers language a social product with a genetic and functional link to all practical activities carried out by man in society. In his view, language is one of the most traditional elements of culture and *the most resistant to change*. This would explain the great effort it takes for the immigrant to change his language, the fruit of the culture that nourished him, which he used from a young age in order to create and assimilate the image of the world around him. A newcomer to a different environment must learn—at great cost—a new language that helps him perceive the specific reality of his surroundings and helps him communicate with others who are part of this reality.

Benveniste has said (1969) that all languages share a certain number of expressive categories that seem to constitute an invariable model. Among these categories are two fundamental units most detectable in speech: *person* and *time*. Every human being fashions his individuality as "myself" in relation to a "you" and a "he." The speaker always refers to himself, the one who speaks, by means of the same indicator: "I." The speech act performed by "I" is always, every time it is reproduced, the same act for the listener, but depending on who performs it, on each occasion it is a *new act* in which the speaker takes part at a new moment in time and in a different texture of circumstances and other speech acts. Each time the pronoun "I" appears in a statement that explicitly or implicitly evokes the pronoun "you," a human experience is renewed and the linguistic instrument comes into play.

Even supposing that the immigrant is in a country where his own language is spoken (although it can never be the exact same language), his speech act will take place at a particular moment of time and in a distinctive set of circumstances different from those he has known. Human experience, product of the dialogues between his "I" and the unknown "you," assumes new dimensions and may even alienate him to some extent, posing a threat to his sense of identity. The threat may grow more real when his habitual linguistic instrument must be replaced by a foreign one if he is to grasp the new reality and try to establish communication with others. The qualities of human communication, fascinating to examine from any angle, are heightened if the communication occurs in a special context such as an exchange between an immigrant and a native. We refer here not to isolated acts of communication at particular times but to the entire communication process with its inevitable mistakes and distortions (attributable not only to imperfect knowledge of the language, but also to the emotional states of the dialogue participants) which develops gradually when contact is made between two parties.

If we examine the epistemophilic impulse in the early stages of life, we see that the young child feels oppressed by the many questions and problems which his mind is not yet able to grasp. A typical complaint a child has against his mother is that "she doesn't answer my questions." Just as she has not completely satisfied the child's oral desires, she does not completely satisfy his desire to know.

The child's complaint plays an important role in his character development as well as in his epistemophilic impulses. It is an accusation that can be traced back to an earlier complaint typical of children that belongs to the period prior to language acquisition and is intimately connected to the first complaint: that they "can't understand what the grownups are saying or the words they use."

The child imbues these two complaints with an extraordinary amount of affect, whether they are made separately or together. If his resentment is very strong, a later migration may cause him to have serious problems in communicating with natives. He may speak in a way impossible for others to understand and at the same time tend to reproduce his original angry reactions when he finds himself unable to understand others. He will be unable to transform into articulate language the questions he wants to ask and will not understand the words of any response directed to him.

The disappointment one is bound to feel when the epistemophilic impulse is aroused in the early stages of development is, we believe, the deepest source of breakdowns of this function. The hatred one may feel for people who speak another language and the difficulty one has in learning a foreign language seem to be derived from the intensity of these first disappointments, as Melanie Klein (1932) has noted. Thus it is useful to apply in these cases some knowledge of linguistics in general and of communication theory in particular, as well as what we know of the feedback process in the circuit of communicative interaction so that we can identify mutual or reciprocal modifications of the message that comes to be exchanged between sender and receiver.

Among psychoanalysts, Liberman (1971) has devoted most attention to research in human communication and the relationship between people who send messages (sources) and those who receive them (targets), who thereby complete the communicative circuit. Using the ideas of modern linguistics, he created an operative model which can be used to evaluate dialogue (the psychoanalytic dialogue), for the purpose of devising a strategy to make communication between therapist and patient complementary.

The theme of the present work does not permit us to develop

these points in greater detail. However, we believe it will be helpful to synthesize briefly some of the principal concepts developed
by Morris, Jakobson, Prieto, Chomsky, and Ruesh, among others, on whose work Liberman based his theories, using Freud's
notion of the "psychic apparatus" considered from the point of
view of its communication and symbolization functions.

Morris (1962), for example, discusses semiotics, the science
that studies the theory of signs. Semiotics is subdivided into
semantics, syntax, and pragmatics. Semantics studies the qualities of signified and signifier that are interchanged between sender
and receiver or attributed to each. The options exercised by each
side in selecting and structuring given signals of the verbal code
in order to transmit the verbal ingredients of the message constitute syntax. (This occurs only if there is a common ground of
experience between the dialogue participants.) Pragmatics focuses
on the relation between the sender and receiver, the signs and
messages they transmit by means of signals. In sum, the manner
in which an individual transmits information to another person
is syntax; the heart of such information is semantic; and the behavior that accompanies the information is pragmatic.

Semiology is concerned with all systems of signs and symbols
that man uses in his communication with others. Semiotics grew
out of the application of semiology to a specific category of signs
in a given field. Prieto (1967), who worked mostly in semiotics,
stated that transmitting a message means establishing one of the
social relationships called "information," "interrogation," or
"order": the sender is the one who supplies or produces the signal, thus creating what is called a "semic act."

The notion of structure in linguistics came about after De
Saussure (1961) distinguished *language*, as a logical system, from
speech, as practice within the confines of language. Through structural linguistics, structural semiology was developed to study the
behavior of signs. Here, some clarification of our terms (signified,
signifier, message, sign, and structure) is in order.

We will use Prieto's illustrative example of a traffic light as it is
seen by the pedestrian. When he sees the red light we say he sees a

sign. In comparing the red light he sees with other red lights he has seen before, he relates the color red to a concept, or *signifier* (a type of sign). When he relates the concept of the color red to the concept of danger, he arrives at the *signified* (a type of message). When he sees a car speeding toward him, he perceives the message of the signal as concrete danger. Thus, in this example the sign is a biphasic entity composed of a *signifier* (color red) and a *signified* (danger).

$$\frac{S}{s} = \text{sign} \frac{\text{red}}{\text{danger}} = \frac{\text{concrete signal}}{\text{concrete message}}$$

To devise a structure we must relate two signs (as a minimum) with opposite and complementary characteristics:

sign 1	*sign 2*
red	green
danger	no danger

Jakobson (1963) identified six factors and six functions that are dominant in any act of verbal communication: "The *source* sends a message to the *recipient*. To be operative, the message must have above all a *context* it refers to, which allows the recipient to be in a position to perceive the message, which could be either verbal or of a nature enabling it to be decoded, transformed, or encoded in verbal form. The message requires a *code* in common, at least partially in common, with the source and the recipient. Finally, the message needs a *contact*, a physical channel, and a psychological connection between a source and a destination, contact which allows communication to be established."

Chomsky's "generative grammar" (1965) refers to a system of explicit, well-defined rules that give structural descriptions of sentences. Chomsky emphasizes that each speaker of a language has learned and internalized a generative grammar that expresses his knowledge of the language. This does not mean that the speaker is aware of the grammatical rules or that his statements about his intuitive knowledge of the language are necessarily true.

For the most part, any interesting generative grammar involves mental processes far beyond the reach of actual or potential consciousness; moreover, it is clear that the speaker's information or points of view about his ability and conduct may be mistaken. Chomsky asserts that the current generation of linguists is concerned with the "creative" aspect of language. The creative aspect exteriorizes "an unlimited proliferation of forms and an independence of expression with relation to pure action whose effects are reflected in an immediate stimulus." This observation led him to assert that "everything happens as though the person speaking, inventing the language as he expresses himself, or rediscovering it as he hears it being spoken around him, has incorporated into his thinking self a genetic code that in turn determines his semantic interpretation of an indefinite series of actual uttered or heard sentences."

In Chomsky's terms, then, the child who learns to speak uses as a basis a genetic code or develops a generative grammar which enables him to "invent" language as he begins to use it or to rediscover it as he hears others speaking it. Anzieu (1976) talks of a "sonorous wrapping" surrounding a child from the beginning of life, just as his skin envelops him, keeping his insides intact. The mother's voice, which the nursing child can recognize after a few weeks, is like milk to the child's ear. It is not insignificant that in the folklore of every culture lullabies occupy a prominent place.

Racker (1952) discusses the specific musical qualities that make the voice have meaning to the unconscious: because of the "unity in multiplicity" principle that governs musical form, the voice may function as a defense and as a means to overcome the depression caused by the experience of losing the mother's protection (in the womb). In the face of the disintegration the child feels when he thinks he has attacked and lost his mother, music, the connection and unification of disparate elements, makes him feel reunited with himself and with his mother.

Screaming and crying, attempts to free oneself from something overwhelming, are linked to all experiences of separation. They are reactions that arise preverbally and reappear when anxiety levels become uncontrollable. They paralyze symbolization and cannot be reduced to words. Screaming and crying are attempts to shake free of something bad, and they become calls to an object which frees one of need, absence, frustration, and pain.

In fact, the first time a child hears his own voice is when he screams. As he begins to integrate the figure of the mother as good or bad, he also begins to organize sounds: he starts babbling, which later changes into words, and words acquire a magical value, for it is with words that the child recreates the object he names, the object he thought was lost. It reappears at his incantation.

In her work in applied psychoanalysis, Melanie Klein (1929) refers to the Ravel opera, with a libretto by Colette, called "L'Enfant et les sortilèges." The plot revolves around the adventures of a boy who does not want to study. When his mother forces him to do so, he sticks out his tongue at her, and she punishes him by threatening not to give him cake at teatime. In response to this oral frustration the boy rebels, breaking everything within his reach and attacking the cat and other animals. Immediately thereafter, all the animate and inanimate objects he has attacked begin to pursue and assail him from all sides. His nightmare ends at the moment a squirrel in the garden falls and the boy instinctively takes his handkerchief to bandage the animal's broken leg. Then he murmurs, "Mama." As he intones this magic word, all the animals and inanimate beings regain their earlier form.

Klein interprets this material in relation to the anxieties brought about by the boy's fantasies of sadistic attacks against his mother. These anxieties are overcome through sympathy and pity. The child learns to love and to believe in love. Colette, with great psychological insight, has the change occur when the child, after curing the squirrel, pronounces the reparatory "magic" word.

Greenson (1950) has also stressed the relationship between language and the mother. He considers speaking a means of preserving the relationship to the mother and also a means of separating from her. Words may be experienced as milk; thus, the child's relation to the mother's breast is a decisive influence on his future relation to his mother tongue.

At the same time that language is what adults use to understand one another, it is the object of jealousy, hate, and passionate desire to the baby, who has only an imperfect understanding of it. This situation is aggravated when the parents have a "secret" language from which the children are excluded, as they are excluded from the parent's sexual relationship.

Just as repressed memories are never entirely forgotten, dismissed languages never completely disappear; they leave traces in the unconscious. Thus, for example, Freud used traces of the old, "forgotten" languages of the child Sigmund, who emigrated with his family from Freiberg to Vienna, to stir up old memories from the time when he was still using those languages.

Freud learned to speak several languages because he had several "mothers" and because in their conversation his parents sometimes used the language of belonging (Yiddish) and at other times the language of reference (German).

Why did Freud become a genius and not a dyslexic? Frequently in cases of multilingualism, as in cases where there is a change of residence resulting in significant modifications in sociocultural, linguistic, and affective environments, the superimposed codes become intertwined and can cause writing and learning disabilities.

If children to whom life or parents have posed problems that are too complex for their age are loved in a way that promotes narcissism and imparts a value to imaginary omnipotence, they more rapidly develop a lively intelligence. They need to understand prematurely—on the one hand, in order to dominate the external conflicts upsetting them and threatening their psychic integrity; on the other hand, to make themselves all the more loved because of their brilliance.

Elias Canetti, winner of the Nobel prize for literature in 1981, gives a masterful description of such a situation in his autobiography, *The Tongue Set Free*. Born in Bulgaria of Sephardic parents, he spent his childhood and youth in Bulgaria, England, Austria, and Switzerland.

> When my father came home from the store, he would instantly speak to my mother. They were very much in love at that time and had their own language, which I didn't understand; they spoke German, the language of their happy schooldays in Vienna. . . . So I had a good reason to feel excluded when my parents began their conversations. They became lively and merry, and I associated this transformation, which I noted keenly, with the sound of the German language. . . . I believed they were talking about wondrous things that could be spoken of only in that language. . . . I repeated to myself the sentences I had heard from them, in their precise intonation, like magic formulas. . . . But I made sure never to let my parents notice, responding to their secrecy with my own. . . . It never dawned on them to suspect me, but among the many intense wishes of that period, the most intense was my desire to understand their secret language. I cannot explain why I didn't really hold it against my father. I did nurture a deep resentment toward my mother, and it vanished only years later, after his death, when she herself began teaching me German.*

Although Canetti's parents spoke German, the language he could not understand, between themselves, they spoke to him in Ladino.

> To us children and to all relatives and friends, they spoke Ladino. That was the true vernacular, albeit an ancient Spanish, I often heard it later on and I've never forgotten it. The peasant girls at home knew only Bulgarian, and I must have learned it with them. But since I never went to a Bulgarian school, leaving Ruschuk at six years of age, I very soon forgot Bulgarian completely. All events of those first few years

*Elias Canetti, *The Tongue Set Free*, trans. Joachim Neugroschel (Seabury Press, 1979), p. 10.

were in Ladino or Bulgarian. It wasn't until much later that most of them were rendered into German in me. Only especially dramatic events, murder and manslaughter so to speak, and the worst terrors have been retained by me in their Ladino wording, and very precisely and indestructibly at that. Everything else, that is, most things, and especially anything Bulgarian, like the fairy tales, I carry around in German.

I cannot say exactly how this happened. I don't know at what point in time, on what occasion, this or that translated itself. . . . I can say only one thing with certainty: the events of those years are present to my mind in all their strength and freshness (I've fed on them for over sixty years), but the vast majority are tied to words that I did not know at the time. . . . It is not like the literary translation of a book from one language to another, it is a translation that happened of its own accord in my unconscious. . . . German for me was a later mother tongue, to which I have an indissoluble bond.*

Despite this, in his period of adolescent rebellion, Canetti claimed Spanish exclusively as his mother tongue, "defying the authority of a geography professor, defending the correct pronunciation of the river 'Desaguadero' from the professor, a German, who thought it should be pronounced 'rio Desagadero,' eliminating the sound of the 'u.'"

If we linger over this text it is because it illustrates with all the enchantment and vigor of a poet's voice the importance and weight of the childhood experiences with language that lie in every person's past.

Lacan (1953) maintains that language predates the appearance of the subject, and also engenders it. He maintains that the definable human environment is neither biological nor social but linguistic. In this sense his ideas approach those of Chomsky, who emphasizes that language is not a "mechanical" form imposed on the subject from without but rather an "organic"

†Ibid., p. 26

form, like a seed budding within and progressively attaining the full development of its nature. Language is a system that generates rules and principles which offer finite means to reach infinite possibilities. Moreover, Chomsky insists that language makes order possible in the world. Above all, it functions as the organ of thought, conscience, and reflection, granting the spirit and the mind autonomy over experience.

One of Lacan's most important contributions is the value he places on the concepts of signifier and signified. He defines the signifier as the totality of language's material elements, linked by structure; it is the material support of speech. The signified is the common reaction to everything about an experience that is related by speech. The signified and signifier are overlapping relations. There are two networks; that of the signifier is the synchronic structure of the material of language, whereas that of the signified contains the diachronic totality of speech. The signifier has autonomy from the signified. Language has the possibility of meaning something apart from what it actually says, and that determines the autonomy of the signifier with regard to meaning. In Lacan's view, metaphor is the principal agent of this relative autonomy, but he gives equal importance to metonymy, the replacement of one term by another on the basis of proximity—a connected sense between two terms. Metaphor and metonymy are absorbed in condensation and displacement, respectively, two mechanisms most characteristic of unconscious functioning.

Language determines one's knowledge of the world, of others, and of oneself. It provides a basis of support for one's identity. A child's conscience becomes awakened and broadened as he progresses in language learning, which little by little ushers him as an individual into society.

One must wonder to what extent an adult immigrant can function as a child again, learning to speak, "inventing" language as he expresses himself, or rediscovering it as he hears it spoken around him. We believe the immigrant in general has a harder time than a child identifying with his environment and letting the new language sink in. When he tries to learn it, the adult tends to acquire vocabulary and grammar in a rational way; but not accent, intonation, and rhythm—that is, the "music" of language—as a child does.

When confronted by a new, not-understood language, the immigrant feels excluded, like a child who does not understand the secret language of his parents. In this sense, the experiences Canetti describes could well be those of newcomers to a country who react to the strange language with jealousy, hatred, and a desperate desire to acquire it, in order to be able to participate in a world that appears closed to them.

Immigrants' young children seem to overcome the problem of assimilating a new language more easily than adults, not only because they are more receptive to imitations and identifications but also because of their intense desire not to be different in school or on the street. Often, this gives rise to conflict between the parents and the child, when the parents feel surpassed and criticized by a child who is ashamed of their lack of fluency in the new language.

Some persons show a marked facility for assimilating a new language which, besides being a specific talent, may have to do with defensive motivations. Thus, for example, Stengel (1953) remarks that some immigrants assimilate the new language quickly as manic overcompensation for the anxieties inherent in the new situation. In other cases, the person is fleeing from language and primitive objects which he experiences as persecutory, since his native language is closely linked to more primitive fantasies and feelings. One patient, a native Austrian, used to say, "In German the word 'urinal' smells of urine."

In contrast, other individuals put up strong resistance rooted in dissociative defenses to learning a new language: they maintain that their mother tongue is the only authentic one and the best suited to expressing life experiences, and they scorn the second language as poor and unequal to the task. This reaction may arise from a feeling of guilt at being disloyal to one's parents' language.

Once this resistance is overcome, progress in language acquisition reaches a certain plateau, variable for each person, the middle ground between an imposed environment and one's internal resistances. Sometimes a feeling of shame is attached to the use of certain idiomatic expressions since this is viewed as "penetration of the natives' secret language," which will always be veiled in mystery to the outsider. Yet there is also an unconscious fear of the magic effect of language: the immigrant holds back from using certain expressions as a patient might resist analyzing his dreams: it is as if he feels he is being forced to regress to the very creation of language.

Meltzer (1973) also refers to the "limits of language," citing in this connection Wittgenstein, who tries to define the limits between what can be said (that which can be represented in a "linguistic game") and that which can only be shown, given the possibility that the limit may move as new linguistic games are invented.

For Wittgenstein, language is no more than a game with which man tries to transcend his solipsistic position in the world, his alienation from other human beings, and his ignorance of nature. According to Wittgenstein, a speaker probably formulates the following: "Not only am I saying this, I mean something by it. When we consider what happens in us when we *mean* (and not only say) words, we have the impression that something is connected to these words which would otherwise lack meaning. It is as if by our saying these words something was awakened in us."

However, people suffer from strong disabilities in this domain; and immigrants, owing to the different circumstances they encounter, suffer doubly. Wittgenstein continues, "Some cannot mean what they say; others cannot say what they mean; in the former cases the aspect linked to meaning is so impoverished that it is impossible to distinguish it from senselessness; and in the latter, it is so superficial as to be useless, and so forth."

Each person's historical context is as important as the linguistic game is unique to its context and unintelligible to those outside its framework. Earlier we mentioned that the new communication codes a newcomer must deal with belong to a context so different from his own that there is bound to be greater ambiguity and contradiction in the information he receives. This is true even in countries where the same language is spoken but where a given word or expression that is of harmless content and common usage in one may have a sexual, indecent, or insulting meaning in the other.

As a result, the communication established by the immigrant with native speakers inevitably contains alterations in the semantic and syntactic fields (confusion and misunderstandings between respective signifiers and signifieds, and improper use of verbal structures), which are echoed in the pragmatic domain through the immigrant's behavior and his reactions to messages sent or received from other dialogue participants. For as long as this lasts, the immigrant feels alienated from his surroundings. Some feel they are "in disguise" when they speak the new language, that they have lost the language in which they feel "authentic."

But when these obstacles are overcome, the immigrant feels that he contains the new language, and that the new does not necessarily replace the mother tongue: he makes space within himself for more diversity, which enriches him and may enrich others.

12

AGE AND MIGRATION

Although migrations produce an impact at any stage of life, they are assimilated differently depending on the age at which they occur: it is not the same experience for an adolescent or young adult with a long future ahead of him as for a mature person with much history behind him.

In determining the effect of migration on children, one comes across problems that are much more complex than those exhibited by adults, for in addition to all the variables that modify the conditions, effects, and development of the migratory process in general, one must take into account the problems particular to the child's age and developmental phase.

In some respects one might think that migration is likely to be less traumatic for a child than for an adult because of certain advantages the child enjoys: his immediate environment consists of few people (this varies, of course, with age); if the family emigrates together, the child's move is made with a protective covering, so to speak, an umbrella that shelters him; the child is more capable of imitating and absorbing new impressions, more open to learning, therefore better equipped than an adult to assimilate a new language, new customs, and so on.

However, a child also has special needs. He has not participated in the decision to leave, and even if explanations have been offered (which does not always happen: this depends on the nature of family communication and the child's age), the child is generally at a loss to understand adult motives for moving. In addition, although by emigrating together the family may act as a shock absorber of new stimuli, the adults closest to the child are themselves unsettled by the same migration.

Some people who have experienced migration as infants bear the consequences for the rest of their lives.

In the course of treatment, one man who suffered food phobias discovered that when he was a few months old his parents had temporarily emigrated to Morocco for work-related reasons. The mother, a European woman, reacted to the new country (where she had not wanted to move) by developing an intense aversion and distrust toward everything that came from there, blaming the country's primitive character and poor hygiene. In trying to protect her baby from "poisoning," she spent more than two years feeding him nothing but canned foods that she had brought with her from home. One can easily appreciate the many repercussions of this behavior on the baby's later life.

A similar case is the clinical history of Marisa, detailed in chapters 4 and 5. Several months old when her family first emigrated, she lost all affective connection to her mother as a result of the migration. Although the mother cared for her and even breast-fed her for a needlessly prolonged period, she did not pay enough attention to the baby because of her own intense depression. Thus, a symbiotic attachment (only the mother's milk was "trustworthy") was intensified at the same time as the affective distance increased (the mother was always thinking of other things, or was elsewhere, "in another country").

Erikson (1959) considers that the first and crucial task of the ego is to firmly establish permanent guidelines to resolve the conflict between "basic confidence" and "basic distrust." In his view, the amount of trust derived from early childhood experiences seems to depend not upon the provision of absolute amounts of food or affection but upon the quality of the relationship with the mother, which interacts with the child's receptive capacities. He believes that mothers create a sense of trust in their children by combining caretaking, adjusted to the newborn's individual needs, with a firm sense of personal confidence, within the framework of their own culture and life-style. This is precisely what emigrating mothers lack, and even more so if they are exiles: their sense of personal confidence is in crisis.

As described thus far, the entire premigration period, although its character varies depending on whether the migration is voluntary or nonvoluntary, is a time riddled with doubt, fear, and sorrow. Sometimes the child witnesses bitter family arguments; sometimes he shares with the parents situations of anxiety and panic or becomes the target for the parents' aggression as they take out on the child the anxieties they cannot contain. At other times the child is forgotten by the parents, who are submerged in their own problems, hardships, or depression.

To this constellation of factors one must add, as in the case of an adult, any previously unresolved conflicts, the quality of relationships the child has been able to establish with his internal objects, and the unconscious fantasies that surface during the migration itself.

After arriving in the new country, the child goes through his own process of mourning. Because of his dependency, he also experiences his relatives' mourning, for the family structure that protects him is a shaky one.

Some young children who emigrate are deeply affected by the absence of those who had made up their environment-at-large: friends, classmates and teachers, grandparents, uncles, and aunts, neighbors, as well as the objects belonging to the nonhuman environment: house, toys, parks, and so on. Sometimes, unable to express sorrow, the child expresses anger. Thus, one boy of six, talking of his friend, suddenly burst out, "I think it's shitty Enrique didn't come with us!" Afterward he added, "Why doesn't my father have a job yet?" In this way he associated the two principal sources of his anxiety: acknowledging his loss as well as the fact that his parents had not yet recovered from the regression into which migration had plunged them and thus were unable to help their son or be role models to him. The boy had temporarily lost his father in the role that father had always fulfilled for him.

Despite everything, if previous conflicts have not been excessively serious and if the child's relation to external and internal objects has been sufficiently positive, he will eventually become integrated in the new surroundings, although he will experience the painful vicissitudes of migration: encounters with a new environment, new school, friends, strange cultural mores, being the "new one," the "different one," and so on.

If the contrary is the case, the child will exhibit maladjustment in a variety of ways, depending on his age: he will cling overemphatically to his mother, manifest phobias, retreat into isolation, reject school, inhibit his own abilities and have learning problems, feel beset by his schoolmates' mocking or scornful attitudes toward his different manner of speaking or dressing, or because he doesn't understand the codes of behavior and communication; and he may try to reverse these roles by becoming himself more scornful, ironic, critical, or aggressive.

In other cases, symptoms are expressed more directly in the body, indicating the child's regression and depression: loss of appetite or, conversely, voraciousness; nightmares and other sleep disorders; compulsive masturbation; enuresis, encopresis; changes in bodily functions and propensity to illness or accidents (traumatophilia) in which the child has a tendency to repeat situations that were traumatic for him or acts out melancholic minisuicides.

Clinical examples illustrate some of these situations, which in each case exhibit individual characteristics.

Graciela emigrated with her parents at age two and a half from a Central American country to Spain, under the pressure of adverse circumstances: a sudden, violent political change put her family's life in danger, and they fled into exile. During the period immediately preceding the emigration, the family's anxiety level was at an extreme: the father left first, hurriedly; the mother, who was pregnant, had a miscarriage; and everyone was anxious and aggressive, including friends and relatives. Mutual toleration was at a nadir.

Before that time, Graciela had had some problems: her most significant past events had been a cesarean birth, a serious postpartum operation on her mother for gallstones, and Graciela's refusal to stop breast-feeding or change to solid food when she was old enough to do so.

During their migration, Graciela was in the process of acquiring sphincter control. A short time before, she had learned to control urination during the day but not yet at night. The learning process halted with the family's flight into exile. Because the problem persisted, her parents came in for a consultation when Graciela was five years old. In this regard her development had not been retarded, but her progress was inhibited. Her language functions had developed, but in the new country she used language in a new way, at times becoming regressive, especially at home with her parents. The parents also complained that she was very "demanding," although they used the same word in describing the many nurseries and schools she had attended in their country of origin. After migration they also changed their daughter's schools frequently.

What emerged from Graciela's parents' presentation of the facts was that they felt guilty for having subjected her, through a multiplicity of compelling circumstances, to excessive "demands" for her young age. Now, however, it was she who was not accepting the current demands on her such as not to wet her bed or to separate from her mother and go to school. She had a difficult time fitting in with her classmates since, she said, from the start the other children laughed at the way she drew pictures.

Graciela's awareness of her difference from the others overwhelmed her, yet in her first therapy interview she introduced herself with pride by saying, "I am from Central America. I will speak a different language," and she drew her country's flag. From the outset, she showed by these few words her concern for her identity, which she had to reaffirm in a strange place, and her problems connected to communication (language), which she both desired and feared. She used defensively the fact that she was "different" by emphasizing it, just as at other times she tried to adopt a scornful and exasperatingly provocative attitude by using tricks to hide information, such as by saying "I'll tell if I want to," her fantasy of dominating her interlocutor and having him at her mercy.

She withheld information because she wanted to prove to others and to herself that in some areas she could withhold and control things, though she could not do so with her urine at night. At the same time she tried in this way to dominate any person she considered persecutory. Furthermore, she tried to deceive for fear of being deceived and of being subject to hostile use of information, which she attributed to everyone else.

Her initial interview was rich in material. She played three games which clearly condensed her anxieties, revealing a central theme repeated in different forms, variations on the same melody. First she built a house. The conflict came when she had to decide where to put the doors and whether they would be open or closed. She was very distrustful toward those who might come through the doors. As she worked, she made comments like, "This is so no one can come in, because he would say 'I'm on your side' and then be a bad person." When asked to clarify who was on her side she answered, "My father."

In this setup, we see her ambivalence toward her father, her simultaneous desire and distrust in wanting to leave the door open so he can come in but fearing he will deceive her. The open door, her receptivity, becomes an open sphincter which uncontrollably releases urine. Later, her fears revolve around an enemy trying to get in by pretending that he is a friend: the deception may be that the mother comes in place of the father, the father in place of the mother, or that their union is experienced by the child as something bad rather than their being the desired good parents.

Graciela kept making her house bigger so that more figures could fit in it, as if she were trying to grow, to be able to retain more urine and more anxiety, but the problems with the doors reappeared, as much with a back door as with a side door, which she repeatedly tried to close, with great difficulty.

Clearly, she was expressing in fantasy as well as in her body the terrifying experiences of the pre-exile period, when the house was always in danger of being invaded by powerful enemies against whom the family could not defend themselves—enemies who could trick, force, harm, or kill her, her father, and her mother.

In the second game the same theme recurs, but all the feared figures are joined in a mythical childhood figure: the wolf. She tells the story of the three little pigs, dramatizing it with toys: the wolf pursues them and they escape; the wolf "says he is the mother, but they know he wants to eat them" (again, fear of being the victim of deceit); the wolf tries to enter the house through the chimney, but they prepare a pot of boiling water, in which the wolf burns himself. After this, Graciela asks for a glass of water.

The third dramatization is of the Little Red Riding Hood story. "The mother gives her a little basket of food for the grandma." She relates the meeting with the wolf, who "fools her, making her believe he is the good grandmother . . . but he eats her." The hunter cuts open the wolf's belly, saves the girl, and fills the wolf's insides with "stones." Then the wolf becomes thirsty, goes to the river to drink, and is pulled under water by the weight of the stones and drowned.

The Red Riding Hood story seems to be the story of Graciela's cesarean birth, in which the hunter (father/surgeon) had to take her out by operating on her mother, who, in Graciela's fantasy, had eaten her and did not want to let her out. Even the substitution of stones seems to be connected to the gallstones for which her mother was operated on after Graciela's birth, an operation in which the mother nearly died. On the other hand, Graciela identifies with the wolf, who is dying of thirst, and after she tells the story in which the wolf gets burned, she asks for a glass of water as if to calm her excitement.

In Graciela's case, then, enuresis fulfills several functions with regard to her unconscious fantasies: it saves her from the wolf, who wants to eat her (she burns him with urine as if with hot water); it saves her from drowning inside because she wants to drink like the wolf; and it saves her from what she wants to eat, from which she refrains. At the same time it satisfies her fantasy of admitting the wolf to her pot (the father's penis in her genitals) but eliminates the danger and the guilt.

Deceit is the leitmotiv of Graciela's fantasies: she wants to "close" everything so that "the bad guys can't come in [deceiving her] by saying they're on Papa's side" and yet she wants to "open" so she can escape from the wolf, who, deceiving her, "says he is the grandma, who her mother sent her to see"—a wolf who wants to eat her and enclose her in his belly.

These unconscious fantasies expressed in play explain the meaning of Graciela's symptoms. She is afraid of things "getting into her"—ideas in her head (new language), solid foods (which she refused to chew), and penises in the vagina (she drew herself as a masculine image); yet she is afraid that if she closes herself off she will not be able to escape and will be eaten up. Therefore she opens so that she loses control over her contents, urine and anger (like the mother who miscarries).

In sum, owing to her intense claustro-agoraphobic anxiety, Graciela cannot give up enuresis, which, for the time being, is her only possibility of "escape" and her defense against the terror she feels as being very real, that of being deceived and killed.

Migration caused a sharp increase in the paranoid anxiety that she exhibited as fear of deceit: fear of anything in the new country that could come in from outside and be false, and fear of anything that might give her false insides (wolf/grandmother, who is also an enemy in the guise of a friend). Her deep distrust of new things and the new country, as of the analyst, had its roots in her early childhood experiences, in which a "good" country became a "bad" country (they left suddenly) and the good mother became the bad mother when she fell prey to anxiety (miscarriage, fear, attack). Graciela's defense to all the above could have been either enclosure ("I'll speak another language") or uncontrolled release: enuresis.

Despite her fear of deceit, treatment was possible in her case. Her achievements were noteworthy because despite her distrust, her desire to "soak up" the truth was very great, and that was what prevailed.

Rony's migration took place under calmer circumstances, having been freely chosen by his parents, but it was nevertheless burdensome because it was the second migration in two successive generations. Rony was the son of English parents who had emigrated to Argentina when they were young. He had been born in Buenos Aires; under European law he was British and under American law, Argentine. His parents, however, insisted that he be British and he associated fear with the fact of being Argentine and tried to avoid the risk of being engulfed by this fear by shutting himself in the house, not even going out to play in the park. In fact, he was afraid of going out to the park. At home he spoke English only, although inevitably there were others in the house who spoke Spanish.

While still a newborn baby, Rony had been repeatedly separated from his mother, who was hospitalized for various illnesses; later, she was absent on long trips, motivated by homesickness, during which time Rony was left with grandparents or other relatives.

The feeling of having been abandoned by his parents, difficult to accept for any young child, was harder to bear for Rony because he had so many substitute caretakers: grandmothers and nurses who spoke English, and maids who did not. He developed a variety of fears and acute separation anxiety. When his parents returned he would not let them go out at night or permit his mother to leave him alone for a few hours.

When he was three years old, his parents sought therapeutic help for their son, but because of their exclusive association with conationals and their adherence to that group's norms, they sent Rony to a therapist of British origin, requesting that the therapy be conducted in English since the boy could not express himself well in Spanish. Essentially, this was yet another way in which the parents prevented Rony from becoming a part of the country where he was born and raised.

Rony's analysis began in English and gradually incorporated Spanish. He was showing some improvement when his parents decided to emigrate to Spain. At this time, he was four. The parents' decision to leave Argentina came as a strong blow to the child. Before he left and was made to interrupt analysis, he regressed to the point of refusing all solid food offered to him, accepting only milk, as if he were a baby. His symptoms worsened with the migration, and new symptoms appeared superimposed on previous conflicts: he established a virtually symbiotic relation to his mother, his fears became more acute, producing recurrent nightmares, and he had a fear of falling through the "hole" in the toilet. This last fear manifested when he was learning to control his sphincter muscles and degenerated into encopresis.

Besieged by anxiety and remembering his previous experiences, the child asked to see a psychoanalyst, saying, "I want a Dr. Harry, who took away my fears." Thus he was trying to recover something familiar and lost.

His symptoms expressed his difficulty in mourning the repeated early instances of abandonment, his recent losses, his fears of being abandoned again, and his confusion between two cultures he could not assimilate, a problem now aggravated by the addition of a third new culture, which made the others seem more persecutory. He could not exercise control over his mother, who "ran away" from him, over the country or the people he had lost, or over the new language, all of which was represented by the feces he could not "contain."

This, in turn, was linked to intense feelings of guilt, which made him attribute his previous and current losses to his having ignored the restrictions placed on his use of the other language and culture: if he lost his feces, he feared, he might also lose his genitals.

Thus, for the child, migration, each time it occurred, was a loss equivalent to the loss of his mother; as he was very small, he experienced the loss as a body loss, which increased his castration anxiety.

Encopresis was his way of expressing anxiety, depression, and impotence, his experience of being empty and dissolving into pieces because he had never felt "contained" by his mother. He had always had "many pieces" of a mother: grandmothers, aunts, nurses, and various maids. In the new country he was afraid that the dispersion of people in his life would be even greater, with unknown and frightening figures.

Throughout his treatment, the themes that surfaced most frequently in relation to migration had to do with language confusion and differentiation, as when he interjected English expressions at times of great emotional tension. His most primitive desires were expressed in English, as were the most severe prohibitions: "Bad words can't be said in English."

During one period he drew what he called maps to locate Argentina, Spain, England, and "all the countries where English is spoken," which were all "his." Here, too, dispersion was evident: he had no definable country, or many at the same time.

After many ups and downs, his encopresis receded, along with his fears. Interestingly, a period of retention followed before he learned to regulate his evacuation, and this coincided with a trip the family took back to Buenos Aires.

Some time later, when Rony no longer needed to express his feelings through his body, he was able to verbalize his emotions, and he said that he would have preferred to stay in Buenos Aires but that he would also have been sorry not to return to Madrid.

He was an intelligent child. As he worked through his primitive conflicts, overcoming those connected with his migration, absorbing the parents' culture, that of his native country, and that of his country of residence, he was able to become part of his environment with less fear and less arrogance and to use his knowledge-acquiring abilities brilliantly, without obstruction.

Tempting as it may be to interpret the diverse responses to migration at different ages on the basis of Erikson's (1959) well-documented epigenetic development scheme, one must admit that the scenario is always much more complex than it appears and subject to many variables which make each case unique. In the above cases we have seen the rich significance of pathologies derived from migratory experiences. However, the symptoms displayed by Rony and Graciela, even granting their diversity and nuances, could also be related to the anal-muscular maturation stage during which the migrations occurred.

At that age, in general, a child needs to experiment with his objects in two modes: holding and letting go. In either one of these modes, his basic conflicts may appear as benign or hostile attitudes. Holding may come to mean cruel restrictions or may on the other hand be a way of caring for objects. Letting go may come to mean releasing the destructive forces that are attacking and emptying the self or a relaxed permissiveness, a "letting be." These attitudes are not in and of themselves good or bad: their value depends on whether hostile attitudes turn against an outside enemy, another person, or the ego. Failures in the child's ability to let go or hold on at will, to create distance or move closer, affirming his autonomy and control, generate shame and doubt.

Early shame and doubt, feelings accentuated by migration, undermine the basic confidence a child acquires, all the more so if his confidence is weak owing to previous conflicts. Shame is a feeling that is easily absorbed by guilt. However, it has its own characteristics. It specifically relates to a situation of being exposed and being aware of being seen. One feels that one is seen in a situation in which one would prefer not to be seen. Shame is an awareness, through others, of one's own incompleteness, nakedness, or imperfection. A person who is ashamed would like to force the world not to look at him so that people will not see the state he is in, and he feels intense anger if he cannot do so. This was particularly observable in Graciela's case.

Doubt, according to Erikson, is the sister of shame. Clinical observation shows that doubt is linked to the awareness of having a front and a back (concretely, a "backside"). The body's rear surface, with libidinal focus on the sphincter muscles and buttocks, cannot be seen by the child and yet can be dominated by the will of another person. Thus it can seem to pose a threat: someone or something can penetrate and dominate it, or it may empty itself without asking permission.

If something important like a migration occurs at the time the child is trying to assert his autonomy and his ability to control, when he is struggling against shame and doubt that he can really do it, one must assume that the child will experience the migration as something that has been "forced" upon him by his elders.

Parents may be voluntary or involuntary emigrants, but children are always "exiled": they are not the ones who decide to leave, and they cannot decide to return at will.

Children of emigrants are exposed to situations which arouse shame: feeling "different" and being unable to compete with children their age (sibling rivals) in the use of language, secret languages, and complicity in cultural codes. As a result, they are full of doubts: who are the good guys and who the bad, the capable and incapable; who is worthwhile, and what is he worth?

Oedipal jealousy and rivalry and their inevitable aftereffects failure, castration anxiety, and guilt also become accentuated in migration. The mother, in the boy's unconscious fantasy, emigrates to follow the father and does not consider the harm it may cause the child; the father, in the girl's unconscious fantasy, emigrates to offer security or well-being to the mother without considering the girl's suffering. Hostility and guilt toward one's progenitors can grow very intense, and, as we have seen, these emotions may be manifested in any number of ways. The children may feel left out and may think their parents, individually or together, are concerned only for themselves. In cases where the child witnesses the parents' divergent desires with respect to emigration, he may form an alliance with one parent or the other, depending on the predominance of a positive or negative Oedipal fantasy, with the result that guilt and fear become directed toward the excluded parent.

In the latent period the child normally distances himself from his early love and hate objects, gives up his desire to hurriedly be a father or mother, and substitutes for this desire to make babies the desire to do things and achieve things with tools and skills. He learns to work and to produce. The danger at this stage is that the child may feel so inadequate or inferior that he loses faith in his ability, and his relationship with friends, the solution of his Oedipal complex, may be retarded and he may consider himself condemned to mediocrity or mutilation. Some children's development is interrupted when family life has not prepared them for school life.

Migration, and to a greater extent exile, accentuates this danger since the child is placed in a school setting that is not only a broader society than that of the family group but also a field in which he has to find, carve out, or fight for a place of his own against wholly adverse conditions: being the "new one," the "intruder," feeling that the knowledge he has is without value in the environment and that the knowledge he lacks could prove valuable, suffering initiation rites which are often cruel and humiliating. This is why in the latent period the effects of a migration are most noticeable in the school environment, although the repercussions are inevitably felt at home in reproaches, hostility, and somatization.

One case we had was that of a school-age immigrant who for an entire year refused to pay attention to the teacher. He laid across his open textbook a magazine in his native language, which he read assiduously during class. The tolerant and understanding attitude of his teacher and parents together with therapeutic help which alleviated the deep suffering behind the wall of his apparent indifference contributed to the radical change that took place during the following year. The child was able to develop the talent he possessed in great measure and became the brightest and most popular boy in his class.

Youth is without doubt the best and the worst age for everything, migration included. Statistical studies on the mental health of refugees and emigrants show that the greatest illness rate occurs in persons who emigrate between the ages of twenty and thirty. This is understandable if one takes into account the fact that at that stage of life the central problem is the search for and consolidation of one's sense of identity; and if an event such as migration intervenes, one's sense of identity is thrown off course.

Yet, as always, there are many factors to be weighed, some of which are so influential as to change the configuration of the situation entirely. Things occur very differently depending on whether or not the migration is desired, whether it is undertaken alone or with the family, and what the child's relationship to his family is. The family functions as a protective shield if the migration is desired or is a shared exile; but the family may function as a coercive force if it has compelled the young person to emigrate against his will. In chapter 6 we dealt with the case of an adolescent in such a situation.

A passage from the previously mentioned novel *El jardín de al lado* (The Garden Next Door) (1981) by José Donoso provides further illustration. The author puts the following words of protest in the mouth of a young man whose parents had taken him with them when they emigrated; now he defends himself against being forced to return with them:

> What made him most indignant, he said, was that his parents made him the pretext for returning to Chile, assuring him that they wanted to go back so that he wouldn't lose his roots or lose interest—as indeed he had, but why hadn't they thought of that before?—in Chilean things, or lose touch with the language, his family, traditions. . . . "My roots are in Paris. I left Chile seven years ago. I'm sixteen years old. I've grown up and gone to school in France with French classmates, living as French boys my age live. There are Chilean boys who aren't like me, who follow everything that goes on back home. I suppose because they sense that their parents are more sincere."

The opposite situation is also common, where an adolescent or young adult emigrates on his own, leaving his family or fleeing from them. The prognosis in these cases varies: if he is really attempting to flee from himself in the illusory belief that all he has to do is change his surroundings, a disastrous outcome can be predicted. His lack of containment and support may precipitate psychosis, perversion, delinquency, or drug use.

It remains true that adolescence is also the age at which it is possible to undertake a migration as part of a life adventure, in which one seeks to discover new truths within and outside oneself or to live up to great ideals. No time of life is better suited to such a journey. As Freud said in a letter to Martha, "We have all been noblemen passing through the world as prisoners of a dream." If these dreams include the adventure of migration, it will have better chances for success if it is undertaken with others who function as a peer group and who help to anchor one's drifting sense of identity by offering solidarity, cooperation, and containment.

Emigrating or going into exile as a young person or mature adult is repeatedly referred to throughout the present volume. We will add no more to the discussion under this heading except to say that migration brings in its wake not only personal problems for the emigrant but also fears, guilt, and a sense of responsibility toward his dependents—his children and the following generation.

Many migrations made in maturity are efforts to overcome midlife crises. They run the gamut from vain attempts at illusory rejuvenation, always fated to fail, to the need to do something new, to develop a still-latent talent, fulfill a previously postponed desire, discover new interests, or foster the development of new creative outlets.

Finally, migration is also possible, though less frequent, in old age. Migration during old age has its own problems and significance. An old person in general does not wish to move: it is painful to leave things that give him security; his past is much greater than his future; he always loses more than he gains. If he moves or emigrates because of adverse circumstances or to follow his children so as not to remain alone, he is very unhappy: he feels regressively dependent, like a child, but without a child's expectations and growth potential to reach new achievements. If it is true that every time we say goodbye we die a little, one dies a great deal in this case, more so if one makes an "involuntary" migration as an older person.

The other type of migration carried out in old age is a return home by the emigrant who has lived far from his native land. This is usually a voluntary migration, a return home to die. By so doing, the older person leaves what he has done and lived in one place to go back to his own. Here, too, leaving has much to do with dying; it is a prelude and acceptance of one's own death.

13

MIGRATION AND IDENTITY

It is widely recognized that an individual's capacity to remain himself during periods of change is fundamental to his sense of identity, which he experiences emotionally. Establishing a sense of identity means maintaining stability in the face of changing circumstances and life cycles. But how much change can an individual tolerate before it works irreparable harm on his identity?

The establishment of a sense of identity depends most importantly on the internalization of object relations and their assimilation by the ego. The ego assimilates objects by means of authentic introjective identification, not by manic projective identification, which creates false identities and a false self.

Events such as migration, which cause drastic change in a person's life, can pose threats to the sense of identity. Victor Tausk, who introduced the term *identity* in psychoanalytic literature (1919), maintained that just as a child discovers objects and his own self, so an adult in his struggle for self-preservation frequently repeats the experience of "finding himself" and "feeling like himself." The immigrant in his struggle for self-preservation needs to hold onto various elements of his native environment (familiar objects, music, memories, and dreams representing different aspects of his native land) in order to be able to feel like himself.

In all his writings, Freud only once used the term *identity* (1926), and he gave it a psychosocial connotation. In a speech in which he tried to explain his connection to Judaism, he spoke of "obscure emotional forces" that were "all the more powerful the less easily articulable they were" and of "the clear consciousness of an *inner identity* based not on race or religion but on an *aptitude common to a group* to live in opposition to and free of the prejudices that undermine the use of the intellect" (our emphasis). Thus, Freud refers to something in one's core, one's interior, that is crucial to the internal cohesion of a group.

Erikson, commenting on Freud's statement (1956), deduced that the term *identity* expresses "the relation between an individual and his group," suggesting a certain consistent sameness and shared character traits. Later we shall return to this point; for our purposes, the idea that one's sense of identity is developed through one's connection to others is fundamental.

In a previous work, *Identity and Change* (1971), we introduced the notion that one's sense of identity is born of the continuous interaction among spatial, temporal, and social integration links. We have had ample opportunity to study these links as they appear in the patient-analyst relation. What follows is a synthesis of the complex permutations that set the stage for the acquisition of a sense of identity in the psychoanalytic process; from these we may infer the ways in which identity comes to be formed and how its disorders affect individual development, the relation between the individual and society, and, most important, the individual's experiences of change.

One must start from the premise that a patient generally comes into analysis with conflicts that to some degree affect his sense of identity. Indeed, it is our view that one of a patient's conscious or unconscious motives for seeking analysis is the need to consolidate his sense of identity.

The sense of identity expresses, preconsciously and consciously, a series of unconscious fantasies which, once integrated, constitute what could be called the unconscious fantasy of the self.

Obsessive and schizoid personalities mark the two extremes along the spectrum of identity disorders; the former possesses a rigid and inflexible identity, the latter an excessively weak and fragile one.

The process leading to the acquisition or maturation of one's sense of identity begins, in fact, with the psychoanalytic process, for the analytic framework itself provides a "container" to hold and keep within bounds the projections made by "pieces of the self." The container, at the same time, becomes the crucible in which complex operations are performed on these pieces before they can become integrated in a whole.

The expression "pieces of the self" is a metaphor describing the unconscious fantasies of certain patients. The fantasies underlie the absence of relationship between various levels of ego repression; the pieces are dissociated parts of the ego, particular roles or identifications with certain objects that function independently of one another, as if they were islands cut off from one another.

Although this image describes the characteristics of diffuse identity, typically schizoid, the container notion is just as applicable to other kinds of identity disorders that afflict patients with clinical neurosis or psychosis.

Another image that helps to illustrate the analytic process and its framework as boundary and container can be found in the notion of the analyst as the arms or, more regressively, the skin that holds together the parts of the baby/patient.

The object relations and identification mechanisms at work in the analytic process and manifested in the transference relation are worthy of attention. Object relations are critical to identity formation because objects are the repositories of intolerable persecutory and depressive anxieties that can become so intense as to prevent adequate organization and stabilization of the ego. Object relations are also the sources of identification mechanisms which are necessary to identity formation and are indispensable points of reference for differentiation. The analyst's container function, together with his interpretive role, allows the patient to work through and consolidate his sense of identity. In this process, the patient accepts the infantile parts of the self and detaches from those regressive aspects of the self that block the path to the firm establishment of an adult self.

On the basis of these concepts we will explore the importance of the three components that in our opinion make up one's sense of identity.

Spatial integration refers to the interrelations among parts of the self, including the physical self; it lends the person cohesion and allows him to compare and contrast objects. Its orientation is differentiation between self and nonself; it provides a feeling of "individuation."

Temporal integration connects the different representations of self over time and establishes continuity from one to the next: it lays the groundwork for the feeling of "sameness."

Social integration has to do with relations between aspects of the self and aspects of objects, relations that are established via projective and introjective identification; it helps to create the feeling of "belonging."

Although for purposes of clarity we have described these components separately, they function simultaneously and interact among themselves. The different parts of the self cannot become integrated in time without being integrated spatially; with temporal and spatial integration, the subject can become socially integrated with others in his environment in a realistic and discriminating manner. We propose that migration generally affects all three types of relations, but depending on the individual and the period of his history, the integration of one or another component may be more profoundly disturbed.

Thus, in the early period following a migration, states of disorganization are common in differing degrees of severity, and these may reactivate very primitive anxieties in the newcomer, such as fear of being swallowed by the new culture or of being torn apart by it, leading to states of panic. These experiences result from conflict between the desire to assimilate with others so as not to feel left out or different and the desire to be different so as to continue feeling the same. These conflicting desires, the mixture of personal feelings and cultures, can cause confusion, depersonalization, or unfulfillment.

A person in this predicament frequently asks himself, "Where am I?" and "What am I doing here?" as occurs when one awakens and still feels half asleep. In extreme cases the person feels alienated from himself, as if he cannot meld the different pieces of his identity. In these disturbances it is the spatial integration link, which corresponds to the feeling of individuation, that is most affected.

Disturbances of temporal integration are manifested as memories in which present events are confused with past occurrences. In its mild form it appears as continuous speech lapses, in which the subject calls people or places by names that refer to people or places in his past. We have already seen that the immigrant needs to bring with him familiar objects of affective significance so that he feels accompanied and can recognize through them a continuity with his past.

Often immigrants decorate their homes profusely with objects typical of their original cultures. The art and handiwork, folk music, paintings, or wall hangings cherished by the immigrant have the effect of anchoring the three components of his identity. Such objects emphasize the difference between the immigrant and the inhabitants of the new country, introduce evidence of the past (the country the emigrant left, where he left his life story), make more palpable his relationship to absent figures, and help him bear the sorrow of being in a place where he has no roots, no history, no older generation (ancestry), and no personal memories.

The danger is that these objects, necessary at first to reaffirm one's sense of identity, will take over all the physical/psychic space and prevent the immigrant from incorporating the new and accepting the past as past. Of the three components of a sense of identity, the social-integration link is most observably affected by migration, for it is precisely in the surrounding environment that the greatest changes take place. Everything is new, it is all unknown, and the immigrant himself is a stranger to the environment. Except in extraordinary cases where special conditions of migration have prevailed, the immigrant loses most of the roles he once played in his community as family member (son, father, brother), member of a profession or the work force, member of a circle of friends, political activist, and so on. As Marisa said, "In the new country no one will know me, no one will know my family, I'll be nobody." Disturbances in the social-integration component result in a feeling of not belonging to any group of people that confirms one's existence.

Migration does not necessarily destabilize one's sense of identity. Sometimes it is chosen consciously or unconsciously as an attempt to establish one's identity more securely through direct contact with the places one's ancestors hailed from, places that because of family stories, reading, or tradition have acquired deep emotional significance and represent one's long-lost and devoutly desired roots. Isidoro Berenstein discusses this idea in *Psicoanálisis de la estructura familiar* (Psychoanalysis of the Family Structure) (1982). At a certain stage in life, every human being goes on a search for his origins, the roots of his identity, and his native identifications. However, the search is not necessarily carried out by means of migration.

Some immigrants such as prominent artists, writers, and professionals can be considered in a privileged category: because of their previous work and background they are already known in the countries to which they emigrate. To continue in the same line of work, maintain one's professional status at the same level as in one's native country, and move in the same social circles secures one's sense of identity.

Naturally, in these cases everything is easier, conditions are more favorable, and the environment more hospitable. The absence of pressing financial problems helps reduce anguish and contributes to better adaptation, as in the case of employees who emigrate for business with all expenses paid, those in the diplomatic service, etc. Yet even so, migration puts one's psychic and emotional stability to the test.

It is only by having a good relation to internal objects, by accepting one's losses, and by working through the mourning process that a person can integrate the two countries, two time periods, and two social groups in a discriminating way. In so doing the person reorganizes and consolidates his sense of identity as someone who remains himself despite changes and restructuring.

14

MIGRATION AND PSYCHOSIS

The structure of the neurotic personality and that of the psychotic personality are more alike than they might first appear; symptoms of abnormal mentality are only an exaggeration of normal manifestations but are not essentially different. In 1907 Freud remarked that "the frontier between the so-called normal states of mind and the pathological ones is to a great extent conventional, and for the rest, is so fluid that each one of us probably crosses it many times in the course of a day."

Any individual or collective crisis which upsets the equilibrium between conflicts and defense mechanisms can set in motion latent psychotic mechanisms, producing psychotic states. Migration, unquestionably a crisis situation, may on occasion cause an outbreak of madness or a slow, inexorable descent into mental illness.

Throughout his writing and especially in his work on fetishism (1927) and the splitting of the ego in the defensive mechanism (1938), Freud points to the irreducible split of the ego in the essential role it adopts toward conflict: on the one hand it recognizes the demands of reality, and on the other it tries to avoid unpleasure. He employed the term *Verleügnung* (disavowal or rejection) to refer to the ego's repudiation of unpleasant reality and reserved the term *Verdrägnung* (repression) for the ego's affective reaction. One of the great merits of this distinction underlining the coexistence within the ego of contradictory functions is its application to psychosis; a milestone in the psychoanalytic investigation of psychosis, it led to the development of the concept —key to the understanding of psychopathological symptoms—of the "splitting" of the ego.

Among the major sources of psychotic organization one finds

the traumatic experience of separation, the child's loss of important objects, such as the mother or mother-substitute, at precocious stages of his development, or the mother's failure or inability to alleviate the child's anxieties. The child experiences great distress and in his desperation feels that he is "falling into the void."

Mahler's description (1971) of pathology in the separation-individuation phase is essential to our understanding of the emergence and development of psychotic states. In normal development, a sufficiently autonomous child can physically separate from the mother and return to her as needed for emotional replenishment in the confidence that she will be there. But if the mother functions as an inadequate container for the child, or if separations are prolonged, the child may have an increased disposition to psychosis.

Winnicott (1971) also emphasizes the importance of a "facilitating environment" consisting of a "sufficiently good mother" to ensure a baby's normal development. In such an environment, a "transitional space" can be created for the child to play in and display his fantasies, and this lays the groundwork for the individual's future psychic and physical health. "Potential space," which according to Winnicott is at the heart of cultural experience (as humanity's common heritage), comes into being only through the child's sense of confidence. If the child is deprived of the possibility of inhabiting such a space, his capacity to play or create is impoverished, and he develops a defensive tendency to form a false self. Elsewhere, Winnicott devises a graphic model to depict the consequences of separation: if the mother's absence lasts for X amount of time, the child can tolerate it without ill effects; if the absence is extended to X plus Y, the child's anxiety may be severe, but he will be able to recover; if the absence or separation is prolonged, however, to X plus Y plus Z, there may be irreparable psychic damage.

Winnicott also refers to the "fear of collapse" that plagues many people and is related to past experience and environmental factors (1970). At its deepest level it is a fear of the self's collapse and the ego's disorganization. Those who have this fear have not progressed adequately in the maturation process owing to a disturbance in the facilitating environment which has failed to fulfill its role of providing integration, support, and object relations. In Winnicott's view, it is erroneous to equate psychotic illness with collapse; psychosis is rather a defensive mechanism linked to an inarticulable, primitive suffering. Fear of collapse can be manifested as fear of death or fear of the void.

An immigrant may experience fear of collapse at the time support seems lacking in his new environment and he feels the impending danger of a free-fall in a state of disintegration. This probably corresponds to what Winnicott calls emphatically the fear of an "*already experienced*" collapse.

The immigrant may be compared metaphorically to the child who suffers a separation lasting X plus Y, who loses significant objects and lacks a "mother" to allay his anxieties: the new country is unknown and cannot always offer the containment and support he had hoped for or idealized in his expectations. Lack of communication—one of the major factors in the onset of psychosis—becomes aggravated in cases of migration in which the subject must confront a new language and unfamiliar customs and behavior. His separation from familiar objects of containment, together with the poor communication he has with the world around him (which limits the "potential" or "transitional" space he needs for "games" and object relations), may permit psychotic aspects of his personality to gain the upper hand, producing severe psychosis. The "crazy" responses of psychotics are a reaction to the "communication" context or, rather, the context of noncommunication that the subject cannot abide. Thus he feels trapped in a system of paradoxes. This situation would be analogous to X plus Y plus Z.

Bateson and his colleagues in Palo Alto (1956) described the paradoxical communication that occurs when one person gives conflicting, or "double-bind," messages to another. The recipient of the messages may respond by ending the relationship in protest at being placed in an impossible situation or simply by indi-

cating that he is not responding. These authors hold that paradoxical communication based on Russell's paradoxes can be seen
in the etiology of schizophrenia.

Recamier (1978) also studied the paradoxes of schizophrenia,
and he categorized as paradoxes not only those psychic forma-
tions that unite two irreconcilable propositions but also those
that tend to invalidate relevant perceptions by labeling them
"crazy." The paradoxes drain of sense and significance the stimuli they receive. Recamier calls the psychic action whereby the
schizophrenic patient drains himself of sense and significance
"inanization" and the tendency to drain the object of its contents
"inanitive omnipotence." In distinguishing between "madness"
and schizophrenia, he underscores the fact that madness is not,
properly speaking, a psychosis but an active strategy to trouble
the spirit and the affects, to make mental effort impossible, and
thus to put the ego out of action. In contrast, schizophrenia is
simultaneously a catastrophe and a defense erected against that
catastrophe. In some types of schizophrenia there is a "psychic
liquification" whereby the ego is shattered. There is a massive
ejection of parts of the psyche onto an object, creating a narcissistic dependence on the object. Psychotic systematization is
anticonflictual and antiambivalent; all defensive mechanisms co-
operate to thrust off the conflict.

Green (1975) defines psychosis as a conflict between pulsion and
thought in which thought is attacked by pulsion. In his view, the
two poles of psychosis are delusion and depression. Delusion is
an activity of hypersignification; in depression, by contrast, there
is a looming void which counteracts the danger of excess signifi-
cation. He describes "blank psychosis" as an empty space which
thoughts attempt to fill but never manage to fill completely: "blank
spaces" remain. A blank thought is related to the concept of object
loss. In blank psychosis, a "blank" invades the psychic space and
generates a kind of windstorm that sweeps everything away. Fantasies do not exist in this space; they arise afterward to fill an
intolerable emptiness. Green's description of psychosis approxi-
mates Bion's concept of "nameless terror," as we shall see.

Bion (1957) postulated the coexistence of a "psychotic person-ality" and a nonpsychotic, or "neurotic," personality. By "psy-chotic personality" he refers not to a psychiatric diagnosis but to a mode of mental functioning manifested in behavior, language, and in the effect it has on the observer. Most characteristic of the psychotic personality are intolerance of frustration together with prevailing aggressive impulses that are manifested as hatred of both inner and outer reality, fear of imminent annihilation, and premature object relations that are set tenaciously in place but at the same time are precarious and fragile. If the intolerance of frustration is very great, the personality tends to avoid all frustra-tion by using evacuative mechanisms, especially pathological pro-jective identification. Such avoidance may jeopardize his contact with reality and in extreme cases may lead to other psychotic manifestations, transitory or persistent. Tolerance of frustration, on the other hand, sets in motion mechanisms which tend to modify psychosis, and contact with reality is maintained. To cope with the prominence of his aggressive impulses, the psychotic per-sonality uses pathological dissociation and projective identification in his protests against internal and external reality so that his principal mental activities—aspects of his self and of internal and external objects—appear fragmented, breaking off into small particles that are violently projected. These particles, called "bizarre objects," are experienced by the subject as possessing an independent and uncontrollable life of their own and seeming to be dangerously menacing from without.

The psychotic patient attempts to use these particles to think with: as a result he confuses real objects with primitive thoughts. Then he processes the objects according to the laws of mental functioning and is surprised that they obey the laws of nature. The psychotic feels locked into a world of bizarre objects from which he cannot escape since he lacks the consciousness that would provide the key to escape. From the remains of the disaster the psychotic will try to reconstruct language, but he cannot form symbols or synthesize words; he can only juxtapose or amass them. He reverts to action when he should use thought and uses omnipotent thought to solve problems more properly solved by action. He cannot dream, owing to an absence or deficit of alpha functions (the function that transforms primitive sensations into available alpha elements in order to compose thoughts during wakefulness, dream-thoughts, and memories). When a psychotic patient states that he has had a dream he is probably referring to hallucination, not to dream phenomena per se.

Hallucination is another symptom clinically characteristic of the psychotic personality. It is an evacuation into the outside world, through the sense organs, of the personality's fragments and of internal objects. In the psychotic patient we find a permanent attack on all the links: that is, object links, links among the parts of the self, links to internal and external reality, and links to perception of these realities. Being besieged, the psychotic gives the appearance of tending to engage in logical, nearly mathematical relations, but these are never emotionally reasonable.

Bion stressed the importance of the mother-baby relationship in his notion of "container" and "contained." A mother functions as an affective container of the child's sensations and anguish (content), transforming them into bearable anxieties. Using her maturity and her intuition, the mother successfully converts hunger to satisfaction, loneliness to company, and the fear of dying to peacefulness. The mother's ability to be receptive and to contain the child's projections and needs is called her *reverie* capacity. If a mother has functioned with good reverie, the child will be equipped to cope with frustrations and separations; if not, the child is more apt to inhabit pathological states and display psychotic phenomena. Psychosis, then, may be attributable to the child's inability to properly dissociate and project. His deficient dissociative and projective mechanisms are often the result of the failure of the mother or mother-substitute to contain the child's projections. Such failure also produces a deficit in alpha functions, which transform the content of sensory and emotional experience into alpha elements that assist in the creation of thoughts, dreams, and memories. Consequently, there is an excess of beta elements, which can be evacuated only via pathological projection. Inability to cushion the impact of sensory and emotional information makes a person more vulnerable to psychotic illness.

Berenstein (1982) believes that psychotic functioning is characterized by disruptive, violent behavior and a breakdown of linguistic-semantic content, whose end result is a dissolving sense of reality. A person interacting with a psychotic becomes perplexed and surprised by the subtle changes in their relations. A decontextualized object becomes mobilized within the psychotic, causing ego confusion and blurring his reality index and ability to discriminate between internal and external worlds. An alteration occurs in the psychotic's ability to understand and be understood, perceive and be perceived, deriving from the ego's emotional experience; self- and mutual awareness of what and how each person perceives break down. There is a sense of unprotectedness, often accompanied by fear of annihilation and of the void.

What all these authors have in common in their perspectives on psychosis is the key role played by object loss, the void, or the absence of the mother (or mother-substitute) who can act as a container. In other words, an emotionally significant separation may contribute to psychosis.

As we have seen, an immigrant also suffers loss and the absence of protective, containing objects and for that reason may become exposed to states of psychic decomposition. His transitional space, one might say, is underdeveloped, and an adequate intermediate zone has not been created to ease the integration of his inner and outer worlds. He generally fails to use what this space has to offer him—the possibility of hope—in order to promote an imaginative, creative attitude toward becoming assimilated into the new world around him. In short, migration tends to touch off psychotic aspects of the personality on the basis of the person's inner disposition; the discontinuity of context and breakdown in communication also play a role.

An immigrant may develop pathology in any form and will present symptoms of varying severity according to the previous condition of his personality, the complexity of his circumstances, the quality and intensity of his feelings of loneliness and helplessness, and so forth. In some cases psychic disintegration takes place a short time after arrival in the new place because the immigrant cannot tolerate the new conditions and characteristics of the environment: they act as unknown, aggressive stimuli that cannot be assimilated. We have seen cases of scholarship recipients and professionals from Latin America and Spain who emigrated for purposes of study or research and after a few months of residence in the new country experienced acute psychotic crises. One patient developed a serious paranoid delusion whereby he believed he was a victim of a conspiracy specifically directed against him by the staff and his colleagues at the institute where he practiced his specialty. He interpreted conversations among his colleagues which took place in English (a language in which he was not fluent) as unequivocal confirmation of his delirious fantasy. He was convinced that he had been chosen by them to kill the president of the United States and that he would later be eliminated to protect the members of the conspiracy. He believed they chose him because he was a recently arrived foreigner who did not know how to protect himself from the criminal plot being hatched around him.

In the case of another professional, migration brought on manic-depressive psychosis. In addition to cycles of euphoric excitation and melancholic depression, he went through periods of widespread psoriasis. Significantly, whenever the psoriasis broke out over his body, his psychotic symptoms diminished, sometimes disappearing altogether, and recurring when the psoriasis cleared up.

To illustrate some of the concepts presented above we offer material from an analytic session.

The patient is a thirty-year-old woman, married with two children, native of a Latin American country, where her parents still reside. She had to leave them when she emigrated for the professional advancement of her husband. The separation from her parents and losses caused by the migration took a heavy toll on her; she could not adapt to her new living conditions and complained constantly that nothing in the new place was comparable to the old, idealizing in her memory all she had left behind. Gradually she fell into a deep depression, which intensified when her husband was sent abroad on business, as happened fairly frequently.

Her intolerance of separation was also evident during weekend and vacation interruptions in treatment. On these occasions she reverted to using rigid obsessive mechanisms to counteract her anxiety. Her state worsened with depersonalization and derealization episodes, some of them prolonged. A clearer picture of the nature of her borderline pathology, related to her migratory experience, emerged in the session transcribed below, in which the patient had a dramatic hallucinatory reaction to a phone call from her husband telling her that his return from abroad was delayed by one day.

> *Patient*: I feel very bad. Yesterday F. called and told me he would be back on Wednesday at noon instead of Tuesday as previously planned. It was rather strange. When I heard his voice it sounded very far away; I felt sad and was afraid when I found out that he was so far away. I had everything arranged and had planned to pick him up with the children. . . . Something similar happened once before. I went to get him at the airport; the plane arrived and all the passengers came out except him. I asked to see the passenger list and he wasn't on it. I got scared. . . . I thought he might have been in an accident on the way to the airport. Then I tried to calm down and convince myself that nothing was the matter, but I thought that when I saw him I would take revenge. When I got home I found a delayed telegram in which he explained why he couldn't travel that day. That's why when he called yesterday I got frightened; when I heard him talking I said, "You're so far away!" Besides, I was upset that all my planning had been for nothing. I was going to go to the hairdresser's early, then pick up R. at school and go to the airport to wait for F. I realize that I always plan ahead. I don't know what good it does to plan things out so much.

Analyst: You need to plan in order to fill the emptiness
   caused by F.'s absence; that way you don't feel so far away
   from him or so alone. Planning is the substitute that keeps
   you company.

Patient: Yes, I remember a while back, when my mother
   came to visit, I cried a lot after she left and started to
   organize and arrange all the things in my house, especially
   the things she had used. Last night I was very depressed
   when I went to bed; I was about to doze off but not yet
   asleep when I had a vision. It was terrifying. . . . I thought
   I saw R. disintegrating, breaking into pieces. . . . It wasn't
   a dream; I was very frightened, agitated, and my heart
   was pounding. I wanted to erase the image; at first I
   couldn't, then I could but I was very scared. I thought
   about you to calm down, and I covered myself with the
   blankets.

Analyst: R. represented you as a little girl; fearful
   that F.'s absence would cause you to fall apart,
   you needed to think of me to make contact with
   someone close by so you could feel whole.

Her husband's absence and her fantasy of losing him definitively
because of his delayed return reactivated in the patient the trauma
and anxiety of the losses brought about by her migration, which
in turn prompted the hallucinatory fantasy of disintegration, projected onto her youngest son. The breakdown of her obsessive
defenses acted as a catalyst for the emergence of the hallucination. She needed to evoke her analyst as a containing object and
use her blankets as a protective, integrating skin.

In this example the patient developed a borderline, predominantly melancholic psychosis as a response to the traumatic experience of migration. The psychotic phenomenon denominated borderline, with its constellation of symptoms (free-floating anxiety,
paranoid attitudes, tendency to depersonalization, deep depression, despair and impotence, feeling of inner emptiness, intolerance of frustration and separations, psychosomatic disorders, and

so on), is relatively common in emigrants who have fragile personalities with latent psychotic mechanisms. Had they not experienced migration (especially in unfavorable circumstances) these personalities might have been able to continue living fairly normally, maintaining a psycho-physical balance, however precarious. But migration and its vicissitudes act on these people like a detonator, exploding the fragile mental equilibrium they have gained, largely by using controlling defense mechanisms, and the abovementioned symptoms result.

Other individuals have an apparently conflict-free period and a few years later experience general collapse, in the form, among others, of a depressive or borderline or delayed psychotic state, or as somatic illness (gastric ulcer, cancer, myocardial infarction, and so on), which we suggest could be considered a "psychosis of the body." One explanation as to why these delayed reactions appear may be that they occur when the person loses the fantasy that the migration is temporary with the hope of prompt return, and it gradually dawns on him—for some it is a wrenching realization—that the loss and separation are definitive and irreversible.

15

THE IMPOSSIBLE RETURN

If there is one factor that clearly distinguishes one migration from another it is whether the possibility exists of returning to one's homeland at a future time. This factor is of great consequence and is independent of the decision to remain permanently in the country to which one has temporarily emigrated, as may occur in the case of a scholarship student, for example, or an emigrant with a one- or two-year work contract, or an emigrant who had left with the idea of permanently settling elsewhere but decides to return home after all. The great difference resides in *the knowledge that it is possible to return*. This stamps the character of the migration.

If the doors are open for an eventual return, the pressure on the emigrant diminishes, and his claustrophobic anxiety decreases; he does not feel he is on a dead-end street; he can enjoy his experience. Later on, he may be plagued by doubt and ambivalence, which may just as easily induce him to flee setbacks or frustration as tempt him to stay and settle if an attractive enough offer presents itself. He may review all the alternatives he considered before leaving his native country to start his adventure.

When a return is not possible, the situation is well defined from the start: once one sets out on the road of exile, there is no turning back, no alternative. Such was the case for most of the Europeans who emigrated to America in the nineteenth and early twentieth centuries. The exceptions were those who left Europe to "do America," hoping to return rich and prosperous, the envy of their families and neighbors. Generally return was impossible for those who fled poverty and persecution, those who had no money enabling them to return, and those who left their countries illegally or to escape extermination during the Nazi era; and it remains true that return is always out of the question for political exiles and refugees.

However, if the involuntary immigrant, despite these conditions, manages to reorganize his life and distinguish between those toward whom his hate and his love are directed, he can form an affective attachment to the country that receives him, whatever his difficulties in getting there have been. The impossibility of returning concentrates all one's efforts in the direction of integration with the new surroundings.

One example of an impossible return can be seen in the case of a patient who at a very young age had emigrated with his parents from Europe, shortly before the war broke out. Whenever he referred to a conflictive or emergency situation in his life he would say, "It was as if they were pulling up the gangplank on the last boat to America." This phrase, part of his personal code, eloquently portrayed the anxieties he had once lived through during the long, dramatic period which fed his claustrophobic fear of "not being able to get out," not being able to save his skin. In his case, the panic of "getting locked in" was a reference to his native country, which had become extraordinarily dangerous at the time; but he recreated this sense of panic every time he felt himself trapped in a situation he could neither control nor get out of. He tended by his actions to create situations time and time again in which he was about to get trapped; and he always saved himself at the last possible moment, as if miraculously. His behavior was in part at the service of a compulsion to repeat derived from traumatic early childhood experience, but he also used it defensively to "recreate the miracle of salvation."

Every migration, as we have said, in some way leaves its mark on the person who has lived through it. The traces it leaves, in their variety and complexity, can perhaps best be studied in a country like Israel, which has had to receive and contain huge numbers of immigrants in proportion to the stable population, over a relatively short time.

Two main groups made up these migrations, each with problems particular to it. The first wave comprised immigrants from European countries who had survived the horrors of war and Nazi concentration camps; the second, of immigrants from North Africa and Asian countries. The impossibility of returning to their native communities was common to both groups, but there were notable differences in culture, language, folklore, customs, intellectual level, and history—and hence in the problems of adjustment to the new country.

Although these groups of immigrants had chosen Israel as the country where they could live freely, securely, and in dignity, their adjustment to it was so fraught with difficulties as to make many of them fantasize about returning home, which they might have done had it been feasible.

A sizable number of the first group of immigrants had been victims of Nazi persecution; many, together with members of their families, had been confined and tortured in concentration camps. Those who survived while their friends and family were exterminated developed a specific pathology later called the survivor syndrome, which has been treated extensively in the psychoanalytic literature of recent years. The common elements in the traumatic history of these persons are loss of loved ones, loss of home and all possessions, humiliation and discriminatory treatment, physical and psychic suffering (torture, seeing others tortured, nearly dying of undernourishment), attacks on self-esteem and sense of identity. These people tended to react with extreme apathy (lack of interest in living) or states of depersonalization, stupor, or terror. After they were liberated and resettled in the countries to which they had been able to emigrate, the full-blown syndrome could be observed: there was an early period of supernormality, followed by a second stage of symptoms such as anxiety, sleep disorders, nightmares, phobias, memory disorders, chronic depression, tendency to isolation, identity problems, psychosomatic symptoms, and occasionally, psychotic disorders.

In treatment it was observed that these patients manifested various tendencies in relation to their traumatic experiences. Some deliberately hid their memories, as if they needed to reject them and dissociate themselves and others from these experiences, thus confining and transforming them into a secret bulwark which was never to be penetrated. Others reacted with paranoia, accusing others of being responsible for their tragedy and feeling that those who could not help or did not want to help were forever in their debt. Still others masochistically dwelt on their experiences, repeatedly and in great detail recounting the story of their sufferings.

The serious ego alterations in these patients have been noted by various authors. Kijac and Funtowicz (1981) point out the simultaneous coexistence of two aspects of the ego: one part continues to live in the concentration camp, utterly defenseless; the other, adapted to the new reality, behaves as though it were capable of loving, working, making plans for the future, and so on. The balance between the two is at best precarious, with the current ego continually being invaded by the ego fixed in the past; thus the syndrome arises.

We agree with Niederland (1968) that the pathogenesis of this syndrome can be understood through a focused study of the sense of guilt in all its possible disguises. The origin of this guilt probably can be found in ambivalent feelings over the loss of loved ones; the guilt is intensified by the fact that the other's suffering and death could not be prevented, and, we would add, by the fact that the survivor survives. Clearly, these feelings of "persecutory guilt" (Grinberg, 1963) intensify the harsh attitude of the superego and explain the masochism of the ego.

One can easily understand how in these conditions the immigrants' assimilation into a new country is thrown into drastic disarray; for them, assimilation means integration into the other world of the living, the nonconcentration camp, the place where they can be treated with dignity and respect and where they can obtain the gratifications that their sense of guilt prevents them from accepting.

The case that follows is that of a person who suffered from survivor syndrome and was treated in Israel. The patient, Austrian by birth, is forty-two years old, married, the mother of four children. She works as a nurse in a hospital in Tel Aviv; her husband is an engineer. She and her family had been interned in a Nazi concentration camp. Her father and younger sister died there; she, her mother, and an older brother survived. She was very surprised that a short time after their liberation, her mother set up housekeeping with another man.

The patient had experienced an early stage of euphoria in the new country but then had not been well. She felt defenseless, had bouts of depression and trouble relating to people, especially to the head nurse—obviously, a mother substitute—with whom she argued frequently, seeing her as severe and arbitrary, like the concentration camp guard.

In her early sessions she told of a love affair she had carried on for a few weeks with a friend of her husband's. She said she had given herself to this man out of pity because he was very lonely. Afterward she felt terribly guilty and told her husband about it; he did not attribute much importance to it.

This event contained several meanings. On the one hand, she had projected her own sense of loneliness onto this man, and she needed to gratify him and show affection because he was, in her projection, the defenseless and affection-starved part of herself. On another level he represented an image of her father, whose death, together with the death of her sister, had left her feeling terrible guilt. But she also identified with her mother, for the very thing she criticized in her: she repeated her mother's infidelity (she had fantasized that her mother had been involved with the new lover even before the father's death), whereby her feelings of guilt toward her father increased.

Her guilt caused her to idolize her father, and she saw only his positive, affectionate, tolerant aspects. Moreover, she admired him for his culture—he had been an impassioned reader. Significantly, her choice of spouse followed a positive Oedipal line, for her husband was also well educated, patient, and tolerant of her whims and behavior. She personally identified with her father's intellectual side and she usually brought with her to therapy sessions the books she was reading.

The analyst's interpretation of her confusion was that she was asking for help in distinguishing her various feelings of love, jealousy, anger, and guilt. All these feelings made her anxious and depressed.

On one occasion she had a memory of her father in which she saw him carrying a bag with objects at the time they were arrested by the Nazis. At that precise moment, it seemed to her that the bag was so heavy it pulled him down. She felt as weak as her father had been at that moment, fearing that the weight of her affects could make her fall at any time. She needed a strong figure to support and sustain her. Her weakness was also her way of denying the strength it had taken to survive.

At a different stage of her analysis, she spoke of strong aggressive feelings against her mother-in-law in particular and her boss. She also admitted to feeling occasional hatred for her mother, her husband, and her children, about whom she had death fantasies. In a dream from that period she was on a tandem bicycle with another person; they had to cross a bridge but the brakes were not working and she was afraid they would not be able to stop. The significance of this dream as a transference fantasy was clear: she was afraid of not being able to control the erotic or aggressive impulses arising during treatment (tandem) and was afraid that the analyst traveling with her could not help her in this regard. Her feeling of desperation deepened when she could not continue to dissociate her hatred by directing it only toward accepted bad figures; she was also directing it toward her loved ones.

Her ambivalent feelings toward her lost loved ones (she remembered being surprised to find herself singing after her sister died) made her feel guilty, as did the fact that she had survived, like her mother (whom she criticized for having survived). At the same time, reparatory tendencies attached to the father figure enabled her to repair herself. She recalled an incident in which she and her sister were walking down a street in their city during the time when they had to wear the Star of David to identify themselves as Jews. Many stores had signs saying that Jews were not allowed. One of these stores had a display window behind which someone was preparing tarts. They drew closer to watch. They were hungry. The person preparing the pastry took pity on them and gave them two tarts, which they ate but felt guilty about afterward because it was not kosher food. What's more, it was Yom Kippur, a religious fast day. When they told their father, he forgave them, saying that under the circumstances they were justified in doing what they did: he allowed them to forgive themselves in order to survive, even if by doing so they transgressed certain rules.

This patient experienced analysis as if it, too, were nonkosher food, but she needed the analyst to give it to her with the understanding that she needed it in order to survive. In the same way she sought a good father to justify her survival and her mother's. To find him, both she and her mother had recourse to sexual behavior and fantasies that were "not kosher"—not socially acceptable.

She mentioned a dream in which she saw that her daughter had to finish washing dirty laundry before getting on an airplane. Her associations with this material had to do with erotic, incestuous, and masturbatory fantasies from her adolescence which became reactivated in transference. The fantasies alternated with recurrent dreams of aggressive content. Taken together, these constituted the dirty laundry she felt she had to wash clean in order to be able to get on the plane, the symbol of her migration.

She was in effect asking the analyst for help in washing away a sense of guilt that she herself could not banish because she had survived with these fantasies intact. She repeatedly expressed the fear that her uncontrollable fantasies could destroy her loved ones. In one dream she saw members of a terrorist group in a shoot-out; on the ground lay pieces of cotton singed by bullet burns, and someone was collecting these to manufacture new ammunition.

In another dream she saw her husband's cousin, demented and incontinent, being probed with a catheter; when the probe was removed the cousin's urine sprayed everyone, including her. She was extremely repulsed. She associated this with sexual symbols and said that her husband at the time was going through a period of premature ejaculation, which made her feel resentful and frustrated.

Analysis revealed that her sadistic sexual fantasies appeared in dreams and that in some way she felt she was the cause of her husband's premature ejaculation: the "pieces of cotton strewn about" would represent the semen that was spilled and lost owing to her own incontinence and inability to control her feelings (the demented part of herself, whose sphincter was out of control), which was "killing" her husband's potency (as well as that of her analyst).

The basic fantasy behind her feelings of guilt was that in order to survive she had to kill others or let them die. Her reparatory attempts were constantly being frustrated: she would dream that she loved someone who was dying or that she loved him after he died.

In the course of her brief treatment, this patient showed considerable improvement: her bouts of depression diminished, her insomnia (fear of dreaming) and migraines subsided, her sexual and emotional relation to her spouse improved, as did her relationship with others. Yet much work remained to be done because her basic conflicts, fueled by her tragic experience in the concentration camp, where she had been subject to great deprivation and extreme defenselessness, persisted.

Berenstein (1982) maintains that the Holocaust was a manifestation of mass social aggression, the effects of which will continue to be felt for generations by victims and aggressors alike. The greatest aggression that can be inflicted on one human being by another is to reduce him to a position of extreme defenselessness that leads to his annihilation. In the camps defenselessness was induced by terribly powerful attack-objects, in the face of which protective objects were weak or impotent. To this was added an attack on the subject's identity, which deprived him of the identifications which had helped him recover, as a newborn, from initial helplessness—psychic and motor incapacities—and his own aggressive impulses. When a prisoner had nothing else he could lose, his name was taken away and he ceased to be a person, becoming a number, one of many; he no longer had any qualities at all and was converted into quantity.

We would add that the survivor, or whoever did not perish under these conditions, later feels defenseless not only on account of the aggression that was inflicted on him, which he fears will be repeated, but also on account of a great sense of guilt arising from his ambivalence toward those who died and his identification with the aggressors: this guilt leaves him disarmed, unable to counter the reprisals taken by his internal objects. Thus, defenselessness not only is related to the external world but is deeply embedded in the inner world, where the subject feels neither loved nor protected. This makes him feel trapped and utterly impotent.

How do people who survive such conditions experience subsequent migration? Any situation which creates a state of personal defenselessness and endangers one's sense of identity is experienced as an aggressive act and activates the fear of a recurrence of past suffering. People in this situation will not be able to mix well with the group that receives them in the new country unless they have overcome, at least in part, feelings of guilt for being alive and unless they have recovered, even partially, basic trust in human beings.

Among the vast literature on this subject is a novel, a jewel of its genre, called *Enemies: A Love Story* (1972) by the Nobel prize winner I. B. Singer. In it the author describes masterfully and not without humor the adventures in the life of a concentration-camp survivor in the United States, the country to which he emigrates.

First the reader sees how the protagonist's experiences literally turned his world upside down, changing him from an honest, educated, conscientious citizen into a "criminal element" for being a Jew. After being stripped of his job, social standing, family, and property, he loses the right to exist. A Polish peasant woman who had been employed by his family as a servant saves his life by hiding him in a barn. Their previous roles are reversed as his life becomes completely controlled by this woman, on whom he depends in an increasingly regressive state.

Finally they escape together to America and settle down as a couple. But his confusion and paranoia make it impossible for him to adjust to the new country or to feel integrated as part of a couple. While forever blessing and expressing his gratitude to the woman and to the country, he compares everything he sees and every bite he eats to "before," in the idealized Poland of his childhood. Through the new country and the new wife he relives the fear and distrust of Nazi-dominated Poland. He lives in isolation, not wanting people in the neighborhood to know him, does not make friends, and so forth. Then, in the city where he resides, he runs into a former lover, with whom he shares past, culture, intellectual level; his wife, by contrast, is a good woman but common and illiterate. He begins to lead a double life in which he repeats actions and gestures from the time he spent in hiding, when he had feared being discovered. He confuses his feelings toward each woman and lives on the run, lying to both, lying at his job, giving false names so that the existence of his lover will not be discovered by one circle of friends and that of his wife, of whom he is ashamed, by another. He becomes increasingly perturbed, quits his job, and talks about losing his mind.

The drama culminates when his ex-wife, whom he thought had died in a camp, reappears. The guilt that had been latent becomes embodied in her, one of the "living dead" who terrifies him, making his already untenable situation intolerable and precipitating his tragic end.

It has been said, and it would seem to be true, that survivors of massacres such as the Holocaust and the atomic explosion of Hiroshima inevitably become so disturbed that in their mental states they are like people from another planet.

16

EXILE, A SPECIFIC KIND

OF MIGRATION

Thus far we have analyzed the complex, painful emotions involved
in all migratory experiences, whatever their nature, and the hard,
searching work it takes to resolve the conflicts migration brings
to light. One may assume that exile makes the same experiences
all the more intense and heartrending. Uprooted from home and
surroundings, the pain of defeat still fresh, and his heart sinking
for all he has lost, the exile often must leave without so much as a
goodbye to friends and family.

Saying goodbye is in the strictest sense a ritual act that, according to Sánchez Ferlosio (1983), serves to establish "protective
borders." Departure is the border that divides the state of union
between two people—the one who leaves and the one who stays
behind—from the state of separation. The dividing line between
presence and absence, departure creates the tension of belief that
"we will meet again" and the tension of fear that "we will never
meet again." The traveler who leaves without saying goodbye is
spurred on by impatience, a state of uneasiness, and apprehen-
sion. He often tries to compensate for the missing goodbye later
by using the telephone to allay his anxiety and to exchange the
messages "thank goodness you're home" and "thank goodness
you called." To hear the other's voice has a calming, reparatory
effect. A goodbye places a protective shield around the frontier
that is crossed by the departure. It is a protection that implies the
hope of seeing each other again yet also contains the fear of never
seeing each other again. When misfortune strikes, goodbyes are

the first thing one clings to with all one's heart and soul in an attempt to understand and accept the tragedy of separation. The rite of farewell virtually stamps the incomprehensible with a watermark that locates and orients one during a critical moment. The first thing consciousness needs to know is where it is now, where it is going. The rite of farewell is a marking device which clearly fixes a border between what has been called from time immemorial the land of the living and the land of the dead.

Generally, exiles are denied the protective rite of farewell. Most often they must leave suddenly and abruptly. In addition to other anxieties, they carry away with them the anxiety of not having said their goodbyes, which makes them feel that they are crossing the frontier between the land of the dead and of the living. At the deepest level, all the loved ones they could not say goodbye to and whom they fear they will never see again become transformed into the dead, from whom they cannot achieve a satisfactory separation. And they feel that they, too, have become dead to others.

Exiles are compelled to live far from the countries they fled for political or ideological reasons or because exile is their only means of survival. They cannot return to their homelands as long as the causes that drove them away persist. Herein lies the difference between the vicissitudes and evolution of exile as compared to those of other migrations: for the exile, departure is imposed and return impossible.

Although the term *exile* is widely used to refer to involuntary departures as well as to so-called transplanted, displaced, and stateless persons, it was originally associated with the Athenians, who banished certain citizens for political reasons. Exile was taken most seriously by the Greeks; it was seen as a strict sentence, harsh punishment, true condemnation.

In our day, of all the problems stemming from civil war and violent upheavals around the world, exile is one of the most serious: it segregates important sectors of the population from national life, forcing them to adjust to unwanted, hurtful, and frustrating situations.

Many exiles suffer from survivor syndrome as detected in prisoners of Nazi concentration camps who managed to survive while family members and friends were tortured and exterminated in the gas chambers. Similarly, exiles can be swamped by the guilt they feel toward companions who died. Such a state of mind is fertile ground for skepticism and disillusionment, if not utter despair.

In the words of the exile writer Benedetti (1982), "Sometimes one's courage is bullet-proof, yet one's heart is not disappointment-proof. Many of the young people who risk their lives for political convictions must learn to acquire the grayer, more modest courage to accept defeat, confront a reality different from the dream, begin to build a daily life for themselves."

Exiles experience integration and a life-style shorn of the ritualization they were accustomed to as the loss of a defining identity. They feel insecure, out of sorts: it is even harder for them than for other immigrants to find a place in the new society since they cannot reproduce under the new conditions that which had been the axis of their lives.

The exiles' predicament in the new country is many-faceted. They did not travel toward something but were fleeing or expelled from something, and they are bitter, resentful, frustrated. To face their complex problems they may use as a defense the denial of the present, which then becomes imprisoned between a past mythologized life (converted into the "only thing worthwhile") and the future, represented by the illusion of being able to return home: an illusion all the more nourished the greater the impossibility of acting upon it.

In the early stages the exile may feel like a hero, received with sympathy and admiration, or like a guilt-ridden renegade. This works against the possibility of his becoming integrated in the new environment because he experiences integration as betrayal of the cause, of those left behind, of those who died.

Exiles in this category may reject everything the new country has to offer—anything that is different from their own customs, language, work, and culture. Rejection masks their guilt toward those they left behind and disguises the rancor and hatred toward the country which expelled them, which is projected onto the new country that has received them. Thus, instead of seeing the new country as their salvation, some exiles see it as the cause of all their troubles while idealizing their original country with never-ending nostalgia. Sometimes exiles react like orphaned children who have been placed by adoption and then take out their previous suffering on their new parents, essentially because they have finally found someone who will listen.

But hatred is a two-edged sword: it is a vital stimulus if it can be controlled and prudently apportioned, but it is a dangerous, destructive weapon if out of control. It attacks the person's sanity and can destroy the sources of hope and help if the exile masochistically directs his hatred against the very people who have welcomed him, for example, by becoming so demanding that he makes the new environment the target of all his criticism and projects onto it his own inability to give, help, and protect his loved ones.

An inability to give results from the initial regression and dependence which occur in all migrations, as detailed in previous chapters, but it appears to be more deeply rooted and long-lasting among exiles. Sometimes it is manifested by a marked oral avidity and an incapacity to wait: the exile develops a peremptory need for instant gratification.

The tensions of exile affect family life by creating new conflicts or reactivating old ones. Guilt for having involved one's family in such a hard way of life may cause intense suffering; alternatively, guilt feelings may be projected onto the couple, causing mutual accusations of having failed to protect the children by exposing them to an uncertain and difficult future. As Benedetti says, "Since exile flattens and crushes one's life, someone has to take the blame for all the frustration and anguish, and of course it is the closest person who bears the brunt of it, the first closest person you can find."

Such a situation brings many couples to the breaking point or else causes definitive ruptures. Some exiles who were political militants in their countries feel unable to tend to their children's needs. Previously they had not cared for their children because other interests, considered unpostponable priorities, took precedence; now they feel impoverished and defeated and cannot offer themselves as role models. The lack of stability in their lives, coupled with the feeling that they are just passing through (hoping for a prompt return) accounts for the dwindling interest some exiles take in trying to regain their previous social or professional status; by the same token, a lower social standing increases security and feelings of persecution. Their need to work at a variety of trades outside their chosen fields in order to survive and their excessive dependence on others, in contrast to their previous independence, make them feel depersonalized, and it becomes difficult for them to take on any identity other than that of exile.

Even under the best of circumstances, the exile's situation —imposed from without, not freely chosen—is painful and is experienced as a prison term. Some exiles have said that the vast world into which they escape is no more than a prison because they are deprived of the ability to be in the one place they wish to be: their own country. Others who are imprisoned for years at home feel that they, too, are in exile because they are condemned to remain disconnected from their country.

In this connection, an exiled journalist eloquently expresses the exile's dilemma:

> We are condemned to have our children grow up in a language that is not their own, seeing streets and trees that our eyes do not recognize. We are condemned to watch our grandparents slowly die, by mail, and to be told of nephews' births in abrupt phone calls. But perhaps the worst condemnation of all is to watch our country recede from our reach like a foreign, distant, undecipherable tide and to witness how indecisively our bodies begin to seek stability after many precarious years; our bodies, unconsenting and perhaps irremediably, grow accustomed to a country which they did not choose of their own free will.

The words "perhaps irremediably" have tragic overtones. They suggest the anguish a human being feels in the face of the inexorable and unalterable, as in the face of death.

In primitive fantasies, death is conceived as reunion with one's ancestors. The metaphor expresses human concern over where one goes to spend the last of one's life and represents the desire to return to the land of one's ancestors, as an unconscious fantasy of returning to the womb. To die far away from home "in a foreign land" is considered a double death because it makes the fantasized return impossible.

These concerns show up either latently or overtly in the material of patients who have experienced migration, and more so in cases where the migration itself was an exile. Literature, folklore, and popular lyrics offer abundant examples of the sadness of dying far from home, as in the following emotional verse from a tango:

> Lejana tierra mía
> bajo tu cielo
> quiero morir un día
> con tu consuelo.
>
> Homeland of mine so far away
> beneath your sky let me
> die some day
> with you, my consolation.

The following personal narrative of a professional man from a Central American country provides moving, eloquent testimony of an exile's experiences. His reflections are so sincere, dramatic, clear, and heartfelt as to make commentary on our part nearly unnecessary.

One day my wife came to the office with an unusual message; a friend and highly trustworthy person had been told that my name was at the top of a hit list of university professors to be assassinated by order of the government. This happened two days after a friend and colleague of mine had been kidnapped, brutally tortured, and murdered.

The information precipitated a dizzying period of several hours of rushing back and forth looking for a place where I could hide; a way was found to get me out of the country, and I was taken to a plane (where I met another man whose name was on the list); and it ended with the sudden abandonment of everything that had made up my way of life.

During this time I lived through an intense mixture of facts, feelings, and thoughts; though I managed to adapt partially and temporarily to the circumstances, they left me no time to think about the future or reflect on the past and present. I was in an unreal situation, practically a dissociated state in which I functioned as a passive observer of things, reacting to them only if they represented an immediate threat to my life. For example, after the doors of the plane closed, takeoff was delayed for about twenty minutes; at the time my friend and I were overwrought with fear and anxiety, based on our suspicions and distrust. Subsequently we learned that our fears were not unfounded, because the delay had indeed been caused by a last-minute attempt to remove us from the plane. During the trip, unremarkable in itself, we went through emotional extremes that swung from initial relief to the rapidly dawning awareness of the reality of exile. At first we were filled with nostalgia over what we were leaving behind and over our luck; and we also thought about the future of those who were keeping up the fight, with whom we rather enviously identified as if to compensate for the uncertainty of our own futures. Then a chance encounter with another colleague who was traveling on the same plane, on a pleasure trip, eased our anxiety for a while, since we talked for a long time about trivial matters. However, our worries resurfaced when we arrived in the city of our destination.

On the ground, we kept an eye out for cars that might be following us, which only showed the nervous and fearful state we had been living in, but our thoughts were concentrated on getting to the apartment so we could call home and tell them we had arrived safely and to ask after family friends. This thought made us fear for their safety in a series of imagined scenarios.

Two days later I met with others in the same situation. Together we started the process of mourning, with many long discussions about possible solutions which offered the least number of changes and the prompt recovery of all we had lost; but we also tried to deny our loss by establishing our headquarters in the offices of an international organization, which we somehow saw as an extension of our countries.

But this illusion was bound to give way to a recognition of reality, and so after I wandered about, mentally and physically, in search of the past, I realized that I had to do something to survive, so I started looking for work. It was an important decision because by making it I took the first step toward a possible solution of my problems.

If the choice of my country of refuge was in part fortuitous, my choice of the city where I was going to live and work was related to my past history and an ongoing personal mourning process. It offered me the opportunity of recovery, and by finding a job I was also able to begin planning for a family reunion.

I think that emigrating is more than simply moving from one place to another; actually it is a complex phenomenon that can be studied from so many different points of view that one runs the risk of forgetting that it is one picture with diverse quantitative manifestations. At any rate, emigration is without doubt an act that has a profound effect on the individual, the people around him, and their shared environment.

I have emigrated twice and on both occasions to the same country. Both times I knew my departure would be for a prolonged period, but this time I am not sure how long it will last; it does not depend on my decision alone. The first time I left I did so voluntarily, with specific goals in mind;

this last time I did not want to leave. I had planned on spending the rest of my life in my country. But my second departure was a question of survival.

Both times I went through identity crises and sadness, and I attempted to recoup my losses. I've felt anger, guilt, and also satisfaction; I've both resisted and accepted the new culture, idealized the old one and its objects as much as I idealized what I hoped the new objects could give me. Yet over time, the quality of my hopes has varied in degree, content, and goals; and the changeable combination of internal and external factors has produced contradictions.

At the same time that I confronted the problem of maintaining my identity, I struggled to change it, because when I de-idealized my task I could accept the "bad" aspects of my old culture and incorporate the "good" aspects of the new without completely renouncing my previous identifications. All this helped me to make the required adjustments so I could live in a society that was essentially similar to my own.

One of the major problems of separation has to do with living and dying, processes in constant dialectical movement. In the end, when there is a separation, the possibility of death looms closer and one struggles to ward it off. To separate means to die in the other person's mind, as well as to carry with you what is "dead" in your mind. This life-and-death conflict—carried out, of course, according to the individual psychodynamic and social factors—determines how one reacts to separation. In any case, the loss makes you look for security, which in this context also means survival.

It is evident that despite the drama of the situation people whose personality is stronger and more balanced, who have more defensive resources, and a greater ability to tolerate pain and frustration and to endure and work through their guilt toward those who were left behind or who died are also those with a greater capacity to wait, accept changes of circumstance, and slowly begin to mourn all they have lost. If the environment which receives them is welcoming and there is someone who can contain their anxieties, they can reorganize and carry out creative work in their new surroundings.

A character in Benedetti's novel *Primavera con una esquina rota* (Spring with A Corner Torn Off) expresses it this way:

> I say you have to start by taking control of the streets. The corners. The sky. The cafés. The sun, and more important, the shade. When you feel that a street is not foreign to you, only then does the street stop looking at you like you're a foreigner. And that's how it is with everything. At first I used to walk with a cane, as perhaps befits a sixty-seven-year-old man. But it had nothing to do with my age. It was discouragement. Back then I had always taken the same route home. And now I missed it. People don't understand this kind of homesickness. . . . I know that at my age it is hard to adjust. Nearly impossible. And yet . . .

Examples of people who do manage to adjust are legion. In the history of Argentina and Spain one can point to the Spanish Civil War, which sent huge numbers of exiles, both voluntary and involuntary, to the coasts of America. In the past decade, political turmoil in many Latin American countries has resulted in waves of new exiles, both voluntary and involuntary, to Spain, reversing previous migrations.

On both sides of the Atlantic, many have remade their lives, healed their wounds, and been sustained by what the new and different world had to offer. The most talented poets, scientists, musicians, painters, professors, actors, and writers among them were able to learn from experience; and, enriched by their experience, trials, and tribulations, they produced work that transcended the borders of their adopted countries.

17

SECOND-GENERATION

IMMIGRANTS

Migration has an impact not only on those who experience it firsthand but also on their children. To study the children is useful to our purposes and will provide a more complete picture of the problem, for the children of immigrants, although born and reared in the adopted country, suffer in one way or another the consequences of their parents' postponed mourning or its pathological development.

To help explore the interesting implications and complex permutations of this topic we will give a brief summary of Dellarossa's work "The Professional of Immigrant Descent" (1978). Our objective in doing so is twofold: first, Dr. Dellarossa's clinical material is highly illustrative of the concepts and perspectives we have set forth in earlier chapters, and second, we wish to pay homage to a dear friend and colleague who tragically disappeared not long ago.

Countries like Argentina, with large numbers of immigrants, present noticeable changes from one generation to the next, over a relatively short time period. In their work, psychoanalysts have occasions to interview or treat professionals and to note that their histories have similar strains running through them. We have all seen cases of doctors whose social, economic, and cultural levels are light years away from those of their grandparents or even their parents.

Earlier we discussed the defense mechanisms immigrants use to counteract the anxieties and conflicts inherent in the new envi-

ronment. In the immigrant groups studied by Dr. Dellarossa, idealization was prevalent with prominent regressive characteristics
—most common among them, orality. Everything associated with
food took on extraordinary importance. Any special event was
celebrated with food, and the dining table, the most important
place in the house, was the central meeting place and unification
of the family. Eating and other digestive functions were the main
topics of conversation; behind these one could easily discern hypochondriacal fears related to persecutory anxieties caused by the
loss of the idealized homeland/mother/breast that provided nourishment. The origin of such fears can clearly be traced to the
individual's early affective ties—or, rather, to the pathology of
these ties.

The immigrants were mostly of humble origin, and all had
gone through an initial period of economic hardship in the new
country. But gradually their living conditions improved, and the
parents' desire was—for the possibility presented itself—that
some, if not all, of their children should go to college. Medicine
was the parents' preferred field. Generally the youngest child
fulfilled this desire with the financial assistance of the father and
older brothers.

The parents' preference for a medical career was due in part to
the halo of magic that still hovered over the image of the doctor,
descendant of the tribal witch doctor; but for immigrants in particular, a son who was a doctor embodied the idealized aspects of
the adopted country, since most of the parents had not had access
to higher education in their countries of origin. Moreover, a doctor in the family meant the availability of a trained person to take
charge of and control the family's hypochondriacal anxieties.

How might a son react to a destiny which set him significantly
apart from the family nucleus? To begin with, like any other
human being, he has his own neurotic conflicts, but to these are
added the aftereffects of the parents' migration and transplant.

Where the family nucleus is well integrated in the environment
and mature emotionally, the migration is worked through in due
course, and the family members will emerge from the ordeal with

their affective ties strengthened by shared experience. Within this framework, a son who is an outstanding achiever will have the support of real external objects, which have projected onto him their most valued aspects; he will also have the approval of his own good internal objects. A medical career under these circumstances acquires the significance of an actualized sublimation which represents the reparatory process and creativity, in place of neurotic and psychotic defense mechanisms.

On the other hand, where the family nucleus has been scarred by illness, pathology becomes apparent or aggravated after a migration. Often the family maintains a certain cohesion in the emergency situation, and as long as it puts all its resources into the struggle to survive, it gives the appearance of a certain level of mental health. The family will place persecutory anxieties exclusively in the outside world—in the real problems it is actively grappling with. In these cases there occurs what we have called postponed mourning or delayed grief. To a certain extent the delay is operative in that the work of mourning implies a withdrawal of interest in the outside world and so makes action all the more difficult.

In some cases mourning is delayed for so long that it passes to the second generation. The family of original emigrants keeps up the appearance of being more or less balanced, but the unacknowledged mourning works as a weight, and a member of the following generation necessarily takes that weight on his shoulders. If within the family framework one of the sons follows the chosen career of medicine, it is in all probability a pseudo-vocation whose origins lie in the son's reparatory impulses of a manic nature. In such a case, achievement, rather than gratifying his primary external objects and repairing his damaged internal image, becomes a destructive act against these objects and is accompanied by its corollary, retaliative persecutory anxieties.

Dr. Dellarossa details a case study in support of this hypothesis. The patient is a gastroenterologist, son of poor Polish immigrants. His paternal grandfather had been a blacksmith, and the patient's father as well as the patient himself were trained in this trade. The father, who had emigrated at a young age, had tried to set up various businesses in the provinces, all without success. Every new enterprise failed, until finally he resigned himself to accepting a mediocre but steady job in someone else's employ.

The mother was a bitter, hypochondriacal woman, constantly oppressed by housework and childrearing. The patient was the third of four children. He was the only one to enter a profession; his brothers were poorly educated laborers, and his older sister eventually married a man of the same type.

The patient is described as a man with rough facial features, unclean hands, and ill-fitting, worn-out clothes. Nothing about him evoked the conventional image of the Argentine professional, who is refined in appearance. His manner of speaking was ostentatiously vulgar, and the coarse expressions he used grew coarser when he was angry; surprisingly, he knew a great deal about classical music and literature.

He was married to a woman who chose to care for their three children rather than involve herself in other activities, which obviously pleased him. The patient complained that his wife was thin and "didn't like to eat." He himself ate excessively. For a time he would go to the nearest pizzeria after every session and stuff himself compulsively until he could eat no more.

Shortly after he commenced treatment it became clear that his life was chaotic in all areas. Financially he was drowning in a sea of debts. To pay these off he repeatedly took out loans at banks or other credit institutions, thus adding to his monthly obligations. Whenever he received additional credit he felt euphoric, as if instead of having burdened himself with further debts he had inherited money or won the lottery. To meet his payments he worked very long hours, as a result of which he rarely saw his family. He was afraid that his wife would tire of the life they were leading and would leave him.

Besides being addicted to loans, he had sudden compulsions to make outrageous and superfluous purchases. From one day to the next he changed cars because of a deal he "couldn't pass up" even if he had stayed at home the previous weekend because he did not have enough cash to go to the movies; he capriciously bought jewelry for his wife, who complained that neither she nor the children had decent shoes.

Consequently he would fall behind on payments of some of his loans until he received a threatening letter. Then, anxiety-ridden and cursing, he would run to one of the bank managers and, staking his status as a doctor as a guarantee of his integrity, convince him to delay legal action. On other occasions he did not pay his children's tuition (at an expensive private school because he wanted to "give them the best") and would be summoned by the administration. Needless to say, he was also late in paying his analyst's fees, which at one point nearly resulted in the interruption of treatment.

His relationship to his parents was characterized by ambivalent submission, guilt, and aggression, the same relation he had with his siblings, whom he rarely saw. They would seek him out if they needed something from him—often money or a letter of endorsement that he, as a doctor, could give them. Despite his own financial problems and the weakness of his ties to his siblings, he always gave them money, knowing that they would never pay him back. Nor would he ever dare to ask them. His mother, always complaining and sickly, never asked his medical opinion but did ask for the free samples he received from drug companies or those he could get at a reduced rate.

These data and other material of his analysis clearly showed that the patient had become his family's idealized object and simultaneously the target of their envious attacks. He for his part felt obligated continually to pacify the family's hostility toward his achievements. In his case, being a doctor was a pseudo-vocation which had resulted from a manic need to repair his emptied and damaged internal objects.

The Major Episode

The patient related that the most traumatic event of his childhood had occurred when he was five years old. His father at the time was embarking on a new business venture, and the family was moving once again to a city in the provinces. For reasons that were never made clear, they decided to take the other children with them and leave the patient behind in his grandparents' house, where he lived for nearly two years. The patient described this event as "abandonment," and for much of his analysis it appeared to be the prime motivation behind his neurosis.

In his third year of analysis an episode occurred that shed some light on his tangled inner world. The session had elapsed in the usual vein, the material was repetitive, and the analyst was frustrated at having tried unsuccessfully to understand it. Toward the end of the hour the patient suddenly fell silent. When asked why, he responded, "I was thinking about what you would do if when I got up I kicked you." The therapist's boredom dissipated immediately, but she was sufficiently perturbed to limit her response to saying that he must have a reason for wanting to kick someone. Thus the session ended.

The following day the patient arrived in good humor and said immediately that the previous day, when he was leaving the office, he had felt very warm and affectionate toward his analyst. This did not seem consistent with what he had said at the end of the previous session, but in light of his personal history and his use of defense mechanisms the analyst—inverting the order of these elements—interpreted that he had felt affectionate at the beginning of the session but had hidden it, talking about indifferent matters until the end of the hour, for fear that the analyst would discover his need for affection and not respond as he desired. The rejection he anticipated—the equivalent of getting kicked—made *him* be the first to make a move by having a fantasy of kicking *her*. Only after doing so could he admit his feelings of affection.

This interpretation had an unexpected and dramatic effect. The patient began to sob like a child. When he could speak again he said, using curses and strong language, that for the first time he realized that he had always been afraid to show affection; he admitted that this had caused great pain to him and certainly to those around him.

While it must have been unusual for a man of his build and manner to cry, what happened next was no less surprising. The discovery of his fear of loving inevitably led him to associate it with his "abandonment" by his parents at age five, but this time he told the story completely differently from the way he had on innumerable previous occasions. Previously he had emphasized that the inexplicable discrimination against him had resulted in bad treatment. This time, however, he evoked that period of his life with nostalgia and colorful, tender images. He described the modest dwelling where his grandparents lived, where he washed in the open patio behind a wooden railing; and he recalled the freezing wind that blew through there in the morning. The house was heated only by a pan with ashes and coal that was placed in the middle of the room. The family sat together and prepared *mate* (a typical Argentine beverage) in the morning before starting the chores of the day. Afterward, his uncles would leave, his grandmother would busy herself in the kitchen, and his grandfather, though grumpy by nature, would engage the boy in a game of cards. The family, though poor, was fortunate in having good food; the patient evoked in great detail the meat-pies and fried eggs and peppers his grandmother used to make. He said, "Everything was of the best quality and we ate all day long. There was a garden next door with vegetables; lettuce and everything on the table was fresh. My grandmother was not a great cook but the dishes she made she made well. *I was never hungry*, and the warmth I felt was not from the heat but because everyone was together and got along. I was the only child, and they all spoiled me."

It was clear after he told this version of the story that the patient had been jealously storing this memory, conserving all its emotional weight by transforming it into its opposite. The same had happened in transference with his kicking fantasy. The time he had lived in his grandparents' house had no doubt been a positive experience, but it was an idealized memory as well. He had little capacity for distinguishing the real and good from an idealized fantasy; they became confused in his mind, and in defense he would revert to the dissociation which he also displayed, as we have seen, in many other areas of his life. His profession did not provide him with enough money to satisfy his financial needs; and so he took out loans which made him feel euphoric as long as they seemed to confirm the existence of an ideal object that could unconditionally satisfy his voracity. The analyst represented the mother who had abandoned him, while the pizzeria outside was his idealized grandmother.

The positive, real experience of having lived with his grandparents at the onset of his latency period surely stimulated his intellectual development. He had transformed intellect into its opposite to protect himself from the guilt he had felt over basking for a short but significant period in the affection he desired while being away from his original family. Unquestionably he had experienced a feeling of abandonment when he *left* his grandparents' house, not when he arrived there; and he must have fervently wished to go on living with them. But the real, positive experience was manically deformed because it coexisted with the abandonment by his parents.

After this episode in his analysis, the patient was able to recognize that debts and the internal, damaged objects they represented were his projective identification with his melancholic father, his hypochondriacal mother, and his disadvantaged siblings; and that neither banks nor credit institutions nor the analyst were unconditional, inexhaustible objects obliged to counteract all his frustrations. When he understood that a loan is a contract between two adults and that it was his responsibility to pay back with interest what he received, he came to the (rather obvious) conclusion that by putting his finances in order once and for all he could considerably lighten his work load and he, his family, and his patients would all benefit.

Following interpretation of his situation, the patient began to control his eating habits; he stopped the compulsive visits to restaurants and pizzerias and as a result lost weight and substantially improved his appearance. Finally, he changed his profession, finding work that was more satisfying to him, which confirmed that medicine in his case had been a pseudo-vocation.

Conclusions

This patient's principal family role models were two: his original, conflictive family unit and his grandparents' family, which was healthier but with which he came into contact later. This explains some of the contradictions in his personality.

His grandparents seemed to accept their emigration and made a pseudo-adjustment by maintaining a certain cohesion and by successfully taking with them the idealized aspects of their country of origin, especially those related to orality, while adapting them to local custom (they drank *mate* together). The effects of dissociation were passed on to the patient's father, who attempted to work through his mourning by being melancholy. In effect he repeated the migration by looking for work first in one province, then in another, but systematically failing.

The patient, though he assumed the role of the successful son, did so through the use of manic and psychopathic mechanisms which broke down and submerged him in confusion.

An incident that had at first seemed unclear became significant. The patient once came to a session wearing his sweater inside-out. The analyst thought this could be considered a faulty act, but the patient explained that it was not a mistake, it was just that the right side of the sweater was very dirty. Later on it became clear that this was a manic attempt on his part to deny the confusion of values in his inner world which had resulted from the mixed identification of his primary family and that of his grandparents. If the dirty side was inside, no one would find out, and everyone would believe the side he chose to show, no matter how crudely the seams were visible on the outside. Thus he transformed something from dirty to clean (in the eyes of others) just as he idealized his childhood experience with his grandparents and guiltily hid it while emphasizing his (clean) role as an innocent victim who resented his parents' abandonment.

The family reacted in accordance with its own level of illness. Instead of projecting onto the successful son his good and valuable aspects, each family member exploited his status as a doctor for personal advantage, for nonmedical purposes (endorsements, discounts), thereby denigrating his expertise as a doctor. The patient himself denigrated his profession by making a show of his status in order to obtain credit or delay legal action, by working harder to cover his debts than to cure his patients, and by still being unable to make a place for himself that was commensurate with his social standing.

This case is an example of one of the possible effects of migration on immigrants' descendants who distance themselves from the family environment while the generation which was originally transplanted has not worked through or mourned the migration.

18

THE POSSIBLE RETURN

Life is a continuous becoming. With each passing day, different from the others, one must recreate what disappeared the day before; but migration requires a person to recreate the basic things he thought were already settled: he must create another work environment, establish affective relations with other people, re-form a circle of friends, set up a new house that will not be an overnight tent but a home, and so on. These activities demand great psychic effort, sacrifice, and acceptance of many changes in a short time. But to be able to carry them out gives one a sense of inner strength, an ability to dream, a capacity to build, a capacity for love.

External acquisitions are the homologues of inner acquisitions, new experience and feeling: the new country and new society slowly become part of one's life, as the old country once was; as time goes by the immigrant begins to belong to the new environment and it to him. Every street corner of the city becomes familiar to him, and he fills each with meaning and memory, associating himself with real-life situations; he is loved: this makes him feel richer, fuller; there are more people and things in the world for him to love. Yet he often discovers simultaneously that his integration goes only so far, that he will never be "one of them," a native; he can share many things, but not all, with those around him, and the converse is also true.

It is at that juncture that he toys with the fantasy of going back to his country, in search of lost roots. (For the moment we are leaving out of the discussion the obsessive or compulsive desire of a tortured nature to return home, which comes about as a result of maladjustment or homesickness.)

In his initial interview with an Argentine analyst in another country, an Argentine patient offered to pay the analyst's fees only once they had both returned to Buenos Aires. The patient felt "poor" while abroad and "rich" in his own country; in addition, he projected onto the therapist his own fantasy of returning home. The first few sessions he arrived either late or early: he associated this with what he called his loyalty and his (unsuccessful) desire to do what he assumed others expected of him. The therapist interpreted his time problem as a representation of his attachment to people: he acted either to excess or to a fault, going either too far or not far enough; it was difficult for him to strike the right balance in his relation to others and, by transference, in his relation to his analyst.

He admitted that this had been the case since his arrival in the new country. He was aware that he did not know how to act in order to be accepted by the natives, and he concluded that he had to act "loyally." Clearly, what he called loyalty unconsciously meant submitting to those who he feared were pursuing him so as to placate them, just as on other occasions he reacted with loyalty to make up for his disregard and rejection of others.

Later on in his analysis the patient brought up his sister, who had committed suicide in his native country; he felt guilty for having abandoned her and for not having answered her letters "in time." On another level his sense of guilt corresponded to a feeling of "disloyalty" toward his country for having left it. Around the time that this material was being discussed, the patient was considering the offer of a high-level job in another institution. Although the position and salary were attractive, he was unsure whether to accept it for fear of being "disloyal" to his current colleagues.

Through his identification with his son, who had been in a motorcycle accident and had complained about his plaster cast, the patient discovered that he had experienced his migration as an "accident" which imprisoned him and made him want to break free of the "cast."

A while later he entered into a rather deep depression during which he talked about his guilt feelings toward his wife for not knowing how to satisfy her or how to respond to her continuing homesickness and frequently expressed desire to return to Argentina. Analysis revealed that he was projecting onto his wife his own fantasies of going home, which were complicated by his great ambivalence in reaching a firm decision about the return. For example, he could limit their residence in the new country to a certain number of years or make definite plans to return home. He said he felt he was in the "autumn" of his life and had serious doubts about his ability to start over again back home. Significantly, it did not occur to him that by returning home he would be renewing contact with family, old friends, and former colleagues; he saw it not as a return to a familiar past but as a journey to the unknown, a new experience. This contrasted with the manic impression he had given in his initial interview.

Temporary Migrations

Migrations with a built-in, preplanned return (scholarship winners, visiting professors, company transfers, and so on) belong to a separate category: although they have something in common with other kinds of migration, in many respects they are profoundly different.

A new situation produces inevitable anxieties because the familiar things have been lost, and especially because the person fears he may fail to fulfill the goals he has set for himself; but a short-term migration is inherently different from others. Knowing that return is not only possible but certain makes a person see his new experience as something like an adventure, an exciting voyage into the unknown. This feeling is related, in our opinion, to the inner conviction that one's roots are safe: the subject may be far from home and his loved ones, but he does not feel uprooted. He knows where he is from and where his objects are. The parts of himself contained in abandoned objects and projected onto them are secure and not exposed to despair. Therefore, with his persecutory anxieties appeased and the fear of losing his sense of identity allayed, the subject can rest assured, enjoy the change, and be open to new discoveries, knowledge, and experiences.

A preplanned return, in which one discovers abandoned objects and aspects of the self, acts as a calming influence because of the established time limit for being away. This fact is crucial. We have observed that many people who pass the halfway mark of their preplanned time abroad begin to feel they are on their way back home, regardless of the amount of time that has actually transpired.

One patient who had taken up successive residence in several countries remarked that he was haunted by the feeling that he had forgotten things in every place he had lived. He frequently thought he had at his disposal certain materials he needed for his work, only to discover that those items were in another city, not in his native town, to which he had returned.

Young people in general emigrate more easily and more light-heartedly than older people, not only because they are stronger and more flexible in the face of change but also because either consciously or unconsciously they feel that they are not burning their bridges behind them: their parents remain behind, in a place to which they can always return. We have already discussed how age modifies the effects of a migration; being able to return modifies the experience to an even greater degree.

Fantasies of Return

In any migration the subject fantasizes about returning, but these fantasies usually meet with one of several fates: the idea remains as a future possibility and meanwhile acts as a source of secret pleasure to compensate for the persistent discomfort of uprootedness; the fantasies are acted out in sporadic visits; or the fantasies lead one to make concrete arrangements to return.

One patient, upon returning from a vacation to his country of origin to visit his brother, said,

This time it was very hard to say goodbye to my brother. I realized many things that I hadn't been aware of at the time of the migration. It's a relief to admit it but it also terrifies me. It's as if I'm now feeling everything I didn't feel when I left originally: anger, pain, and panic. It's always been easy for me to say goodbye—I say, "See you soon" and then go. But this time I felt like a little boy on his first day of school who doesn't want to go, who wants to stay home with his mother. The city I live in now enraged and frightened me; I thought everyone there has a family but me; they all have one, good or bad, but at least it's a family that exists. Worst of all, I felt like I didn't belong anywhere. I thought about going back to visit my native city, as I've often imagined doing, and I remembered the places I used to live, but they unnerved me: that was where I buried the dead, left absences, everything there is over. To me the "city that once was" is no more.

These and similar sentiments are expressed in Benedetti's doleful verse:

> They say that after nine years everything there has changed.
> They say the avenue is bare of trees, and who am I
>   to doubt it?
> Aren't I bare of trees, without memory of the trees they say
>   are there no more?

Visits

Trips home—and what are they, if not trips?—to "visit" one's country, even when taken for a purpose other than to explore the possibility of returning, are a time of confrontation. The visitor's overt desire is to rediscover all that was left behind, but he also has a great fear of not finding it. It is as if he wants to penetrate the unknowable, to know how things would have turned out if they had not turned out the way they did, so he can confirm or rectify his original decision to leave.

Most important, we return home out of a need to prove to ourselves that all we left behind is still in fact there, that it did not all disappear and turn into a figment of the imagination, that those we left behind have forgiven us for abandoning them, that they have not forgotten us and love us still.

For this reason, trips home are often preceded by dreams of persecution in which the returning emigrant is accused of something real or remote for which he is punished or rejected.

One patient gave an emotional account of the celebrations that had been held for her husband and herself when they went back to visit their native city after a few years' absence. They were invited out, and receptions were given in their honor, but she was struck by the fact that everyone praised her and her husband's appearance, using unusual adjectives to describe them, such as "radiant" and "resplendent," among others.

It is possible that the occasion—the reunion with their friends, seeing that everyone was there, their warm and affectionate reception, being home—made them both look very happy, and that everyone noticed this. However, in our view, the complimentary remarks also expressed a group fantasy concerning "the ones who left." It was as if the period these emigrés had spent away from their native country was another, unworldly time, as though the natives somehow believed that they had been gone for ten or twenty years when in reality they had been gone for only three or four.

At the same time the group was expressing its surprise at the fact that the unconscious hostility they themselves had perhaps felt at being abandoned had done no irreparable harm to those toward whom it had been directed, the couple who left: it had not killed them or made them sick or age as fast as the home group had imagined. Some members of the home group must have greeted the couple's departure with relief rather than hostility; these unconsciously assigned the emigrés the role of scapegoat—he who is sent, as in ancient myth, into the desert weighted down with the burden of collective guilt, the one who is torn (splitting himself) so that the rest of the group can remain at home guilt-free. This dynamic would also explain the home group's uncon-scious surprise. It was as if they were saying, "What, you didn't fill the role you were implicitly assigned? You are happy and radi-ant?" The adjective *radiant* may be associated with the myth of resurrection and the gleaming halo. The home group's surprise at the visiting couple's appearance could also have meant, "You're not dead? Have you been resurrected?"

Return visits arouse other feelings as well. Some people feel very disoriented, they perceive that everything is greatly changed, that nothing is the same, yet at the same time feel as if they had never left. For some, the return trip awakens the desire to stay at home forever; others have the opposite reaction and are reas-sured to know they have a new place of their own; it may be far away but it has become their anchor in reality.

In general, the person who has left is not the same when he returns, nor is what he left behind the same. With the exception of very strong and solid relationships so firmly rooted that they become part of the subject's identity, a reorganization of values and attachments occurs during return visits: one may feel more of a stranger to someone with whom one had shared much in the past, or feel very close to someone who had not been a close friend before.

One patient who returned home to visit and finish packing the personal belongings she had not taken when she emigrated com-mented afterward, "I went to fetch the things I had left behind, but it was very hard to separate the things I could throw away from the things I should take with me: the value of everything had changed. What I had held onto as luxury items, the latest at the time, had become obsolete."

The same thing happens to affections and personal relation-ships: some lose currency, and the value of others remains unal-terable, together with what is noble and authentic. The same patient recalled just one dream from the period of her visit: "When everything was packed away, I found a package I had forgotten. I didn't know what to do with it: I couldn't leave it behind, but I couldn't take it either."

When one departs a place the self is also left in parts: departing implies a partition. This double meaning of the word is significant. The dream seems to allude to the fact that it is impossible to leave with one's self intact. Inevitably, on visits home some things are recovered and others are discovered to be irretrievably lost. Some people, even if their departure was voluntary, experience the loss as having been deprived of their belongings and turned out of their homes. The house that once belonged to the emigrant ceases to be his: other people live there. His place of work is also occupied by others. The things he loved and that belong to him are scattered like parts of the self that have split off and been dispersed, parts he has not been able to reassemble and take with him.

In addition to pain and jealousy, a feeling of strangeness reigns in the visitor; it is as if he were seeing the world from the perspective of the dead. If this grief for others and oneself can be worked through a second time, the visit home provides a valuable experience.

19

THE DILEMMA

TO RETURN OR NOT TO RETURN?

For voluntary emigrés or former exiles, the dilemma of whether or not to return is not easy to resolve. Even for those who ardently desire it with every fibre of their being, for those who have been homesick and cherish the vivid images of their people, their country, for those who have dreamed day and night of being reunited with everything they left behind—the decision is bound to be difficult. When changed circumstances present these people with the possibility of returning home to live out their long-cherished dreams of rejoining their families, many hesitate and fall prey to doubt. Some project their ambivalence onto family members; such was the case of a famous actor who, returning to his country after a period of exile (during which he had struggled to make his way and finally, by dint of talent and perseverance, was successful), was asked, "What are your plans? Are you back for good?" He answered, "I'm not sure. I never thought this [the political change] would happen. It's terrible for me. My children have made their lives elsewhere, they're teenagers now, and I have to consult them. I can't leave it all; it's been too hard to come by. We'll see how the situation here turns out. For the time being I'll continue coming back to visit as often as I can. When all is said and done, *I don't feel like I belong in either place*" (our emphasis).

In interviews conducted with exiled Argentine intellectuals who were undecided about going back to Argentina, the Spanish journalist Maruja Torres coined the phrases "to be in the throes of de-exile" and "the wound of return." The following excerpt is from her article on the subject:

> At first many believed it would not last; others, their throats still parched with terror and their necks saved in the nick of time, closed their eyes to the immediate past and made ready to live again, to raise the white flag in a strange country which did not yet belong to them. Some refused to unpack suitcases or buy new objects with which to furnish their future; others placed an iron lid on their memories and looked for a way to survive. All are now in the throes of de-exile. Because even those who swore they bore no love for their new country shudder now to say goodbye to those they loved in their years of exile. Even those who will stay where they are will have to say goodbye now to others of their circle who are going back. The wound of return is felt by these men and women who originally came to Spain fleeing atrocities; they came with their bare lives, and the guilt of still being alive, and never, come what may, will they ever be what they once were in the country of their birth.

Certainly, a return migration is sometimes as difficult to work through as an original migration, and the former may have just as high a level of personal and family vulnerability.

One of our patients who had lived far from her country for a number of years had overcome many difficulties and made a comfortable, satisfactory life for herself when a political change in her native country created conditions favorable to her return. Her first reaction was euphoria, a wonderful feeling of space and freedom: she had a choice. She felt her country had suddenly grown, it included both her native country and her current place of residence. She liked the idea of going back to her family and the people she knew. Yet gradually her euphoria evaporated, and in its place came a long, painful period of doubt. A few days after she finally decided to return, "not seeing" some stairs when leaving a restaurant, she slipped and fell.

Her analyst interpreted this event as the patient's way of acting out her fear of not seeing what lay ahead, her fear of being mistaken, of exposing herself to harm. The following day she dreamed that thieves entered her house. They did not take her money but took "an old and funny-looking cheese tray that I used a lot and loved," which she had purchased shortly after arriving in the new country, the same country she now planned to leave. Obviously, the dream showed that she had grown fond of her country of refuge, where she had acquired things; having to leave it not only grieved her but made her feel emptied of her contents, as though she had been assaulted.

While packing her belongings, she came down with flu and high fever which sent her to bed for a week. When her sessions resumed, the material she presented had a pathetic quality: "This return trip is harder on me than N.'s death [a person who had been very close to her]. Then I lost him; now I'm losing everything. I have no colleagues, no house, no furniture. . . . The whole family is suffering, the kids are terrible, I have no one to leave the dog with. . . . I'm constantly arguing with my husband. . . . I'm sick. I got the flu when I was starting to pack. I have a fever. I've broken down, I can't move. . . . I overestimated my strength. I regret the decision. . . . My daughter is stupid: she doesn't understand a thing, she doesn't make a move. . . . This is worse than labor pains."

Here the patient effectively expresses that returning home is similar to or more difficult than grieving the death of a loved one. In this period of mourning she feels she is losing all her belongings and the valued parts of her self. The grief surpasses her emotional capacities and becomes extended to the body, somatizing her suffering. A fantasy of disintegration and paralysis overtakes her: "I've broken down, I can't move." She regressed to an infantile stage and her thinking faculties were inhibited: "My daughter is stupid." At another level she feels the decision is as painful as a difficult birth. Naturally, this "birth" also implies her hope of a new birth.

The person who contemplates returning home does not always see clearly that the return trip is yet another migration. When the emigrant returns to his native country he builds up hopes and has expectations of recovering everything he has yearned for. Even knowing that it cannot be, he hopes to find everything—people and objects—just as he left them, as though they had slept the sleep of Sleeping Beauty, awaiting his return.

But the reality he finds is a different one. When he sees the changes in people, things, habits and styles, houses and streets, relationships and affections, he feels like a stranger. Not even his language sounds the same. Colloquialisms have changed, along with the tacit understanding of words, meanings, shared images, and past references, winks of complicity among the initiated—all the sublanguages that make up a language.

Anxiety over the change that awaits him at home is uppermost in his mind. Great uneasiness and fear color the returned emigrant's expectations of meetings and confrontations, as in these lyrics from two famous tangos by Gardel:

> Yo adivino el parpadeo
> de las luces que a lo lejos
> van marcando mi retorno . . .
> tengo miedo del encuentro
> con el pasado que vuelve
> a enfrentarse con mi vida . . .

> No sé si al contemplarte al regresar
> sabré reír o llorar.

> The lights I glimpse that flicker
> so far off in the distance
> are marking my return . . .
> And I'm afraid of meeting
> a past that once was fleeting
> but now is drawing near . . .

> I won't know when I come back
> and look you in the eye
> Whether I'll break out and laugh
> or break down and cry.

Inevitably, new emotional conflicts erupt when those who return meet those who stayed behind, the welcomers of the returning exiles. Neither those who left nor those who stayed at home are the same: everyone has felt the impact of separation, and beneath the surface, each reproaches the other for having abandoned him. Nearly everything must be rebuilt, like a house after a tempest: fallen trees cleared away, cracked roofs repaired, rubble swept away. And as for the structure itself surely a different house is needed, for the returning person inhabits a different reality. The one thing certain is that he will feel a new kind of homesickness, a new kind of grief.

In some cases, paradoxical only at first glance, an emigrant returns to his native land so steeped in the culture and customs of the adopted country, where he lived for years and fully developed significant parts of his life, that he is looked upon as a quasi-foreigner in his country of origin. He may feel so homesick for his adopted country that he identifies more with it than with his own country. He keeps up with friends and activities there, visits whenever he can, cultivates the language and culture, even sends his children to schools associated with the adopted country to maintain his connection to it, often preserved through the next generation like a legacy passed on to his children.

In some instances the return is particularly problematic. Such is the case of Spanish emigrants who have been hired as foreign workers in other European countries. They have to weave a tortuous course between two cultures and two languages, and the ensuing conflicts are often seen markedly in their children. Special institutions devoted to returned emigrants, as they are called, have been created to help these workers readjust to Spanish society. The goal of the institutions is to help them recover a forgotten language, their native tongue, and to remember the second language they learned, thus to secure the gains the emigrant had slowly achieved: enrichment of his cultural estate.

The following letter describes the complex feelings and strange experiences of a return voyage. It was written by a young professional who had emigrated as a boy with his father and broth-

ers from Italy to Argentina and later decided to return to his
native country.

My first contact was when I went back for a visit. It had
been twenty-three years since I had been in my country. The
idea of going back and seeing familiar faces changed by the
passage of time both thrilled and frightened me. Would anything of my past remain? Would I be able to bridge past and
present?. . . I arrived in Rome and immediately went to the
neighborhood where I used to live. The geography of the
place was practically identical, but of course the tenants'
names in the building entrances were mostly unfamiliar. . . .
My reunion with uncles, aunts, and cousins was very pleasant. Perhaps the most moving moments for me were when I
went to the little town where I used to spend summer vaca-
tions as a child, in an old, spacious family house. My mother
is buried there. Unbelievably, a room of the house, which we
called *stanzone*, still contained my childhood toys, exactly
as I'd left them so many years ago!

The feelings one has at times like these are very special
and rare, unusual, new. It was as if I'd wondered, "Where
have I been all the time that you, my toys, have been here?" I
had the sensation of surprise, or bewilderment, of not being
able to believe my eyes. And one also feels pain and sorrow
and nostalgia. Your perception of time is radically changed
and you feel confused. . . . Having survived the shock of
reunion, I began to appreciate the beauty of Italy. I visited
cities I'd seen only in schoolbooks. But now I was there in
person I could touch things and live it. More than once
while walking the streets of Florence, Pisa, Siena, or Venice I
smiled to myself in happiness. You can't imagine the satisfaction I felt when I went up the Tower of Pisa or the clock-
tower in Giotto. "There you are," I said to the tower, "and
here I am, looking at you!" Curiously, Italy was familiar and
unfamiliar to me at the same time. I'd wanted to go back
some day but I didn't think that day would come soon. . . .

But the situation in Argentina had worsened, and after much doubt I decided to return to Italy. Then I went through a terrible depression, such as I hadn't felt in years. The only symptom I didn't have was insomnia. I felt very sad, defeated, had no appetite, and lost quite a few kilos. I think it was about that time that I made my final decision. . . . I understand that deep down, other factors motivated the decision, some that I perceived and others that will remain unknown.

Many thoughts, ideas, reflections, and feelings came into conflict, and the conflict still persists, because of the fact that my friends, colleagues, and brothers stayed in Argentina and in leaving I had to separate from them. I didn't know if I would be able to handle the separation, live with it, digest it. . . .

Now I'm settling in. I think a lot about how to incorporate everything I lived, acquired, and did in Argentina with my experiences in Italy and my current living situation. I fantasize a lot about visiting Buenos Aires, through contacts in the scientific world, working on something with an Argentinian colleague; in short, I think about keeping alive and active the attachments I formed over the years. Will I be able to, or are these things one tells oneself so one can move away?

This material illustrates the host of problems described earlier. Although in any migration, be it a departure or return, valuable things are irremediably lost (how could it be otherwise?), the emigré's world also becomes broadened and enriched because he has embraced objects and affects of both the old world and the new.

20

HUMAN DEVELOPMENT

AS MIGRATION

Using migration as a metaphor, human development itself can be seen as a succession of migrations whereby one gradually moves further and further away from his first objects.

Throughout his life, an individual lives through the vicissitudes, pain, and losses of various migratory experiences. In this chapter we will summarize these experiences as they occur from the earliest moments of life and discuss the unconscious fantasies they contain, the quality of their emotional content, and, above all, the nature of the ties one forms with one's first significant objects. In so doing we mean to delineate how the history of childhood and adolescence has a decisive influence on the kind of migration a person makes, the manifestations of which have been dealt with in preceding chapters.

Birth is the first "migration" in the life of every individual. To leave the womb and lose the continuous, unconditional supply of food via the umbilical cord is a traumatic and persecutory experience for the infant. Among other things, it frustrates him and imposes the need for him to make an effort to seek food.

This first separation awakens various types of anxiety in the child, of which the most terrifying is the anxiety of possible disintegration or total dispersion. The child feels something is missing, a skin of his own that will contain him. Only the nipple in his mouth, in Bick's words, "like a cork in a bottle," or arms that hold him tightly can assuage his terror of crumbling to pieces. Bick (1968) points out that the baby's skin and his primary objects lend cohesiveness to the aspects of his personality which he feels are being torn apart. The psychological function of the skin as a container of the parts of the self depends initially on introjection of a trustworthy external object. But if the containment function has not been introjected by the infant it is impossible for him to have a sensation of "space" within his self, and confusions about his identity will manifest themselves. In an infantile state of nonintegration, the need to find a containing object becomes a desperate search for an object that can unify the diverse aspects of the personality.

Anzieu (1976) emphasizes the important role played by the "sonorous wrapping" that surrounds the infant like an audio-phonic skin, serving the function of helping him acquire the psychic capacity first to signify and then to symbolize. Along the same lines, Bowlby (1960) insisted on the inherent propensity of an infant to make contact with another human being and "become attached" to him. This need, which Bowlby judges is independent of the search for food, is of a primal nature. Ethologists describe survival mechanisms which develop as a result of the specific response (contact) by others of the species.

Against this background, one may draw the analogy that the immigrant, too, in leaving his country—the womb—needs to come into contact in the new environment with an object that will hold and contain him and to which he will try to become attached. One's survival mechanisms break down if something is missing or inadequate in the reception on the environment.

Through physical contact in his relationship to the maternal object, the infant forms a body scheme or body image, one of the bases for a sense of identity. His loss of the experience of "being inside" the mother's womb is mitigated by physical contact, which enables the infant to work through the loss. In time, the other comes to be viewed as an object of experience so that the child can view himself as well as an object.

In the early stages of life an important differentiation occurs when the child learns to distinguish between his own body and the objects outside it. All his experiences lead the child to stop

considering his own body an unknown entity, and thus individuation slowly takes place. At first the infant does not assimilate his
body as a whole; later he becomes aware of the total nature of his
body, and the other also becomes a total object in his world.

The sense of identity is formed through pleasurable physical
contact with the mother, through which the surface of the body
becomes charged with libido and the body is perceived as the
border between the ego and the world at large. In Mahler's
view, the two critical stages of identity-formation are the "separation-individuation stage," reinforced by locomotive experiences,
and the "resolution of bisexual identification" stage, in the phallic phase.

Evolution proceeds in the direction of enabling one to acquire
an ever-greater capacity to separate and individuate oneself from
the mother, and later from both parents. From the first detachment, which occurs at birth, to the attainment of individuation,
the child goes through other temporary or definitive stages of
separation from the body and the breast of the mother.

Weaning, the first experience of definitive loss after birth, evokes
a state of mourning in the infant, which he tries to work through
by finding other means to feel connected, via other physical zones
that can offer satisfaction and via another object: the father's
penis, which becomes a fantasied substitute for the mother's
breast. By including the penis in his fantasy, the child establishes
the triangular relationship with his parents.

The migration from one object to the next, from the breast to
the penis, transfers to the penis the quality of object relation that
had been sustained with the first object. In this sense, what matters is not only how the child has "said a final goodbye" to the
breast but also how he has been able to separate after each suck-
ling. If the mother has good supportive qualities, the child will be
able to carry out the various developmental migrations on a firm
basis, and any actual migrations in his future without subsequent
disturbances. If, however, the relationship with the mother has
been negative and the real father cannot modify that image, the
penis will be experienced by the child as persecutory and castrat-

ing and will lead to passive submission in his assumption of a sexual identity.

Inadequate maternal containment of the baby's projections or oral dissatisfaction may result, among other things, in future symptoms of "unsettledness" and the illusory search for another earth mother or father-environment as idealized containers. Expressed somewhat differently, if in early infancy the mother has functioned as a good container, the baby will feel greater inner freedom to choose between staying or emigrating (if there are circumstances which justify it); in either case, his decision is more likely to be supported by valid reasons in keeping with reality. On the other hand, if the mother has failed in her reverie or containment function, the child may feel compelled to stick it out, in submission to a maternal object or mother-substitute, or else will try compulsively and repeatedly to travel from one place to another in a constantly thwarted search for idealized maternal objects, which will lead him from one failure to the next, though these failures may be covered up by manic mechanisms. In his psychoanalytic study of the baron Munchhausen (1958), Ferrer specifically identifies the manic mechanisms which disguise the grief of migration.

Although the emigrant carries with him the baggage of his previous history, the outcome of his migration does not depend solely on his past. To a large extent, its success or failure is determined by the quality of the environment that receives him.

The weaning crisis posits an inexorable need to give up the exclusive relation with the mother and to accept definitively the presence of the father as someone distinct from the mother and child. To be "distinct from" implies to be "separate from," yet to be able to return to and be with others. In this sense the discovery of the genitals convinces the child that he has an instrument for reencounters. One is better able to separate and distance oneself if one feels one has the means with which to renew contact and become reunited. Likewise, it is easier to emigrate if one knows one can return. When the child stands and learns to walk, he can move away from the objects which he may fear he wants to destroy out of greed, jealousy, or envy; and he can come back to them and see that they still exist despite his fantasized aggression against them, especially in those fantasies accompanying teething. In another connection, learning to control the sphincter enables the child to feel less anxiety over the loss of feces and urine, which are his products and represent parts of himself, because he discovers that he has the ability to recreate them. At the same time, he progresses in the acquisition of language, which helps him recreate symbolically in words cherished objects such as the mother's breast, which he feels he has attacked and hence lost.

When migration is unconsciously motivated by fear of the consequences of strong aggressive impulses toward the people closest to one, and if one has doubts about one's ability to recover from such aggression, the migration, whatever the rationalizations which justified it, tends to fail.

Growing confidence in the ego's abilities, which make the child feel increasingly independent and in control, is the bedrock of a sense of identity since it ensures the permanence and stability of the self over time. In an analogous way, the immigrant needs to believe in his ego functions, especially in his ability to recreate what he has lost (family, friends, home, work environment, investment in a culture, landscape, language), in order to feel that he can maintain his integrity in the future.

The road to independence is long and encumbered with obstacles, yet this is the direction development takes. Each new step can be taken if the child can mourn for every lost or abandoned object relation and if he can devise new forms of relation with the same objects or with new ones. In this sense, play is the child's vital means of repeating pleasurable situations and working through painful or traumatic ones. It is not for nothing that the underlying meaning of a child's earliest games revolves around union and separation, departure and approach, loss and recovery.

The first game, peekaboo, or making things appear and disappear, is begun between four and six months, when the baby covers and uncovers his face with the bedsheets. It is during this period that he goes through a depressive phase, working through his need to detach from the breast, losing the unique relation with the mother in order to sustain a relation that includes the father. Moreover, in the grip of his fantasies, the baby fears that now that he has recognized the mother as a total person and perceived his ambivalence toward her, she may disappear forever. Thus, just as he plays with things, the baby plays with his body, opening and closing his eyes, making the world appear and disappear.

The first universal toy is the rattle, a toy that makes sound appear and disappear. Its origin can be traced back to primitive musical instruments made of hollowed-out gourds with seeds in the interior.

Toward the end of the first year, the child's games consist of putting things inside other things and taking them out, exploring orifices and filling recipients with small objects.

In the second year, as he begins to walk, the child discovers that there are substances which leave his body and are lost; they fall out: these substances are full of meaning for him, and he usually represents them with water, soil, and sand, his playthings during this period. He sees that he can reconstruct or remodel things with these substances, which are similar to his body products. He also begins to show interest related to keeping or constructing things; these are linked to fertility: dolls and animals hold his interest at this time.

After the third year, games become more diverse and richer in content. Most noteworthy is that the child now learns to draw, a way of recreating and holding onto fleeting images—the same function that speaking once served. The child takes an interest in cleaning and creating order and likes to hear stories told in the same way many times so that he can guard against the anxiety of loss.

Oedipal desires are channeled through games in which the child plays the part of Daddy and Mommy, the doctor, etc. The Oedipal conflict forcing the child to move away once more from early love objects is the equivalent of the exogamic migration in primitive tribes, which established totemic laws as a protection against the infringement of incest and parricide taboos. The child becomes obliged through the Oedipal conflict to abandon his interest in the parental couple and become part of a new environment, such as school, where he will acquire new knowledge, new objects, and new rules of socialization.

The new losses occasioned by the changes of what has been called the latency period and the crossover to new forms of attachment reproduce old griefs such as loss of the oral relation to the mother, which is relived with the first loss of teeth and the waiting period for new, more permanent, and stronger teeth to grow in their place.

Games during this period are different from earlier ones; they are characteristically games with rules, representing prohibitions such as the ones now imposed on the child, and they reinforce the child's repression of masturbation and Oedipal fantasies. At the same time, curiosity, which initially centered on the mother's body and then on the child's own, becomes increasingly generalized to include vaster areas of knowledge, as learning takes place at school, where the desire to compete in sports and skilled games also finds outlet.

Adolescence is the time of life during which the child's overriding need is to move away from the parents of his childhood to begin the exogamic search, given the real possibility of consummating the Oedipal fantasy. This in turn implies that the child must renounce definitively the fantasy of winning the mother (or father) as sexual object.

Reaffirmation of sexual identity, which happens with the first ejaculation or the first menstrual period, is the definitive resignation of the fantasy of bisexuality and the sex organ that is not one's own. It demands that the child work through a succession of mourning periods for all he has had to give up: the progressive retreat from his primary group relation, the loss of his child's body, and the loss of his parents, all arouse feelings of loss in the child. The new stage of separation-individuation and consolidation of the sense of identity coincides with a "migration" to a more distant world: exogamy, the search for new idealized figures that can substitute for the parental couple, and the search for peer groups to which one becomes increasingly attached.

These migrations are in no sense easy: they contribute to making adolescence a highly conflictive period during which extensive and variegated pathology may become manifest, sometimes with destructuring tendencies, owing to the emergence of the psychotic part of the personality.

One might be inclined to think that upon reaching maturity, the individual achieves stability and permanently maintains the sense of identity he has acquired, having no need of further migrations. However, each important new situation unsettles him and foments new crises: getting married, deciding to have children, taking on greater job responsibility, assuming new roles, adopting new ideological positions. These and other contingencies demand greater distancing from primary objects.

When an individual feels he has reached the midpoint of his life, he understands that he has ceased to grow and will thenceforward begin to age. Perhaps he feels that he has reached the limit of his achievements, and he begins to be conscious of the inevitability of death. Particular (though varied) fantasies and anxieties attach to this stage of life, which sets off the "midlife crisis" (Jacques, 1966). These may have to do with the body, its functioning and condition (hypochondriacal fears), with economic insecurity and the fear of financial ruin, of being unable to maintain or increase one's earnings, social status, prestige, etc. The individual at this stage must also mourn various losses: the years of youth that have passed and will not come again; the unrealized potential; the things once possessed and lost; things desired but not attained; the time one has lost.

Old age brings yet another developmental crisis—though it may seem paradoxical to call it such—characterized by anxieties related to one's limitations, illnesses, the total or partial diminishment of one's capacities and work opportunities, and the fresh appearance of fears of death.

Although childhood is an evolutionary growth process and old age a degenerative decaying process, there is a line of continuous evolution which all transition periods follow from one stage to the next. This line leads in the direction of achieving and maintaining a state of separation-individuation and a resulting sense of identity.

In childhood and adolescence this process promotes progressive separation from the mother so that the child can feel he is a separate being, different from others and therefore able to unite with others. In adulthood and old age the objective is to sustain the sense of identity one has attained, to continue to be a separate being, different from others, and to achieve progressive separation from one's children without standing in the way of the evolving migrations they need to make.

21

ADOPTION AND SURRENDER

SPECIAL MIGRATIONS

His father was not his father, and his mother not his mother.
> —Thomas Mann,
> *The Tablets of Law*

The adopted child who once had parents he no longer has and lives with others who are not his biological parents is placed in a situation in many respects similar to that of the immigrant who, for whatever reason, has a native country he is absent from and another country where he makes a life for himself. Of course, the reasons for the adoption, and the ways in which the change of family is worked through can take many forms, with diverse results.

It is noteworthy that we refer to the place of residence of persons whose life and activities occur either temporarily or permanently somewhere outside their native country as their "adopted country."

In the eras of mass migration, people traveled by boat and often made friends during the crossing. These were called shipmates (as we said in chapter 8), and friendships were kept up in the desire to reconstruct a family of brothers and sisters in the new country. People sought out other conationals to share with them all the things they had known and lost; with them, one could build a bridge to the future. Finding friends is related to the unconscious fantasy of being born again and needing to depend on the support ("holding") of new surroundings and new "parents" who receive the subject and accept him.

An adopted child necessarily has special problems apart from the fact that he has migrated from one set of parents to another, from one family to another. In the first place, the child does not change parents voluntarily, nor does he take part in the decision, with rare exception. To this one must add the conflicts derived from the child's age and the manner in which the adoption took place; the frequent deception (adoption often becomes a family secret); the child's curiosity and yearning to know about his original parents; the hard task of mourning the loss of the natural parents and the inevitable pain of not having been loved, of having been abandoned, surrendered to others. Moreover, it is not always possible to know about the conditions of adopted children's early lives prior to the adoption, although one can imagine them as painful in one way or another: the children feel they are an unwanted burden, or are handled despairingly by people who know they will lose them forever. Subsequently the children often must cope with the cold indifference of an impersonal institution.

We have seen abundant evidence of adopted children's feelings and fantasies in the cases under our supervision, both in analysis and in diagnostic interviews (called play sessions). The same fantasies are found in people preparing to emigrate or those who have already done so.

Although the problem of migration has received scant attention in psychoanalytic literature, the same cannot be said of adoption, about which much has been written from many points of view. Yet we propose to discuss it here from a new perspective. Our interest in this fascinating topic was reawakened when we had occasion to supervise treatment in cases where the problems of both migration and adoption coexisted. The conflicts typical of each became interwoven, but there were several common denominators.

The cases we will discuss are of parents who emigrated from their countries of origin and then adopted children in the new country, unconsciously attempting to become established through the children. This circumstance colors in a particular way the adopted child's predicament and his reaction to his adoption. While the child inevitably assigns idealized or persecutory qualities to lost objects (parents, country) as well as to new, adopted objects, these qualities take on particular geographic, national, and cultural characteristics, and the child's hostility or warmth toward them varies over time.

Marisol

Marisol's adoptive parents were highly intelligent Venezuelans who for professional reasons had settled in Spain. They adopted her a short while after they arrived; she was two months old at the time. They found her through an institution which keeps no record of the biological parents. When Marisol was seven years old they told her she was adopted, for fear that she would find out by other means. Her immediate reaction was deeply depressive; she took to her bed and remained there in a regressive state for twenty-four hours, acting like a baby, as though dramatizing the unconscious fantasy of being born again. When she returned to her normal state, her mother noticed that something in her had changed. From that time on the child was "disagreeable" to others and told everyone in a provocative way that she was adopted; this was an expression of hostility, especially directed toward her mother, who had been the "bringer of the bad news."

We may safely assume that Marisol's reaction was not due wholly to her new knowledge or the confirmation of something she may have intuited earlier; rather, it was a condensation of pain and protest at having been abandoned, deceived, and misled, for the information as it was conveyed to her portrayed the adoption as unqualifiedly "marvelous," thereby dissociating or denying the negative aspects of her past. All her rancor against her natural parents for abandoning her was heaped onto her adoptive parents, who were there to receive it. The idealized absent parents were transformed in her mind into bad present parents.

Marisol's parents sought psychoanalytic consultation when

Marisol was twelve years old because she had behavioral problems, a very bad relationship with her mother, and frequent problems with girlfriends, whom she would approach seductively and then abandon; or she would let herself be abandoned, repeating this cycle with a new group of friends who always seemed marvelous to her at first. Her parents were aware that Marisol needed treatment, but even in their initial interview they betrayed their conscious and unconscious fantasies about the course of future treatment.

Child psychoanalysts are continually faced with the unconscious (and universal) fantasy on the part of the child's parents that the psychoanalyst (representing the mother) will attempt to steal the child from them. This is expressed as the fear of "losing the child's affection," "losing his trust," and so on. The special characteristics of Marisol's case gave her parents' theft-fantasies double strength in two senses: their daughter belonged not only to "another mother" but also to "another country."

The parents expressed their fear of retaliation by requesting that Marisol be treated by a Latin American female psychoanalyst because, they claimed, "they are the only ones we trust." But, the mother added, "In a few years we want to go back to our country, and a Spanish analyst might seem like her real mother to her." Despite these misgivings, they accepted a Spanish therapist for their daughter's treatment.

Marisol began analysis with the double attitude of "nothing matters in the least" and "everything is terribly important," displaced onto small matters. She was an intelligent, lively child, pleasant and sophisticated in appearance. In her first interview she stated that nothing special was the matter, she just fought with friends but she could work it out, because she already had new ones. In addition to her apparently manic and omnipotent relationships with friends, she denied that being an adopted child had any importance whatsoever.

She seemed to suggest that loss was unimportant, people were unimportant, even mothers were not important: there are always "others." Her goal was to avoid mourning or experiencing loss.

In contrast, low-level frustrations awakened violent and "awful" reactions in her.

A short time after commencing analysis, Marisol had her first menstrual period. During that time she dreamed there were "men driving around like madmen, getting me into accidents that left me crippled." Meanwhile, on the surface, her relationship with her father was idyllic, and the one with her mother fraught with great tension.

We shall not linger here on the Oedipal fantasies and fears of castration that appeared in her dreams, except to point out that her associations indicated that her particular family constellation caused her to personify "good" and "bad" parents in figures who accompanied menarche. Her fantasies about the risks of being a woman involved not having a penis, being wounded, being in an accident due to the irresponsibility of a man driving a powerful machine (the penis) like a "madman," unconcerned for the consequences. The same could have happened to her unknown mother and father.

These ideas rose to consciousness some time later. When she began to recognize that being adopted brought her a host of particular problems, she saw the problem as the existence of two mothers. Only after a while did she "discover" that she must also have had "another" father.

One thing that remained constant in Marisol's analysis, from the earliest sessions, was her propensity to give double-message responses to the analyst's interpretations. She would always say no at first, but then would bring up material that unconsciously confirmed or elaborated on the given interpretation. Gradually she stopped saying no automatically and softened her responses to maybe, rarely, or similar words. Thus she talked about her fear of "losing it all," yet on occasion thought that "if my parents wanted to, they could take it all away from me."

When she argued with her friends and they insulted her, what hurt her the most was that they called her gypsy, which to her implied being dirty, poor, a nomad, perhaps stolen, as in the myth that ascribes to gypsies the habit of stealing little children. The "family romance" can flourish with deep conviction in the minds of adopted children because it contains an element of historical reality in their lives: their ignorance of their true origins. In Marisol's case, being labeled a gypsy made her suspect that perhaps she had actually been one, and that was why she was perceived as marginal, abandoned early and defenseless. Yet on the other hand it reinforced the fantasy contrary to her family romance, that she had been stolen from powerful, eminent parents.

In some measure her adopted parents shared the same fantasy; in their initial consultation they said that although they did not know who the girl's real parents had been, someone had hinted to them that she was the daughter of "an important and good family."

It was most difficult for Marisol to find "her own place" in a group or feel she belonged to it. She always thought, for example, that she had to "choose" between two friends, and she always felt that by accepting one she was betraying the other.

Her relation with her analyst was on the surface cordial and polite. She defended herself tooth and nail from recognizing feelings of transference, especially her own dependence and need. However, on one occasion the analyst had to cancel a session, and in the next one, the patient brought in material having to do with fights with her mother and a girlfriend because they had deprived her of things. Marisol was furious with her friend because the friend had brought a ball to school to play with and then took it home, saying she was feeling sick, and never brought it back.

In this way Marisol expressed her indignation over the missed session; but this episode in itself repeated the infantile trauma of having been abandoned by her mother. In fantasy, in order to view her mother as a less aggressive and persecutory figure, she justified her abandonment by attributing it to the possibility that her mother had fallen ill. She objected because the mother, like her friend now, had presented a breast that was later withdrawn; still, she seemed to be deeply attached to her need to justify her mother's actions (as she always justified the analyst's interpretations) so as to improve the image of this internalized maternal object.

Immediately thereafter she said her hamster had had babies; her father had suggested that they be drowned since, he said, hamster mothers sometimes eat the babies. Marisol admitted that she had cried when he said that; she associated the event with herself, and for the first time in a session expressed some feeling for her original parents. She said, "They could have done that to me: it was better that they let me live."

But she had a bad dream: "A black cat was in a pit and was eating meat, hungrily. There were snakes too. I had a baby and I threw it in." In this dream we can see the resurgence of repressed material: despite her efforts to improve her mother's image, this image appeared as a devourer, and her only defense was to identify with the aggressors.

In the following sessions Marisol talked about how her mother often accused her of "burning the pan" in which something had been cooking. In all groups she felt that she was "one too many." It appeared that she was afraid of being considered a "bad girl" because she might be "un-adopted." Her fantasy was that she was a bad girl for having burned her mother's pan, as though she felt personally responsible for the sterility of her adopted mother, whose organ of reproduction and nourishment was out of order, as if someone had stolen her "good babies," which in Marisol's dream she had thrown to the meat-eating mother figure. On other occasions Marisol felt that her mother blamed her for "having to feed her" because "cooking is hard work." She projected onto her adoptive mother and her analyst (who did not look after her outside the scheduled sessions and who had once cancelled an appointment) the experience of her natural mother, who "blamed" Marisol for being born and found it "hard work" to raise her.

Her analyst's interpretation of this experience was the first one Marisol did not reject outright by saying no. She answered, "I don't know; sometimes I think so . . . but no. . . ." However, her subsequent associations brought up the hamsters again. She had to give them away; and she added, "They were like me, they didn't spend a long time with their mother—only two months. . . . Their eyes weren't open yet, and they didn't even realize they were with their mother."

With this comment it seemed she was expressing the unconscious perception that she was adopted at the age of two months. She had been told only that she had been adopted shortly after birth, and she did not know that she had spent time in an institution. She did not know why exactly but she "hated institutions like boarding schools." In a similar way she had said, "They were like me; they didn't spend a long time with their mother—only two months."

One of Marisol's frequent complaints was that her adopted mother "interferes" and "takes me for a fool." Her rivalry with her mother and with other girls was focused on "not being taken for a fool" but, trying to get others to "look like fools." In effect, her anecdotes about daily life made it clear that she not only provoked the situations in which she was rejected but also, without realizing it, involved a third person in all her relationships, whom she would later accuse of interfering. Marisol came to recognize the fact that she had tried to get herself expelled from school. At times she initiated intrigues among her friends by calling one on the telephone and pretending to be the other friend instead of herself. On other occasions she lied about her age.

Such behavior, to a certain extent typical of puberty, was more accentuated than usual in Marisol's case; she needed to deceive just as she herself had been deceived, to take others for fools as she felt she herself had been by not being told of her origin until the age of seven. Even after she was told, she continued to feel like a fool; she needed to interfere and let others interfere in her life, just as had occurred in her past history; she needed to reject and be rejected, for that is what had happened to her. All this caused her even greater doubts and confusion and put more obstacles in the way to acquiring a sense of identity.

Her name (so important and significant as representative of one's identity) was the same as that of her adoptive mother. This was consistent with the customs of Spain, the girl's native country, but at the same time her name emphasized that she belonged to a Venezuelan mother. What name would her Spanish mother have given her? Did she name her at all? Marisol's age was also uncertain: her birthday was celebrated on a particular day, but had she really been born on that day? When and why had her parents given her up for adoption? When, where, and how had her current parents adopted her?

At times Marisol admitted feeling sad when she felt unloved, and she expressed nostalgia for the house and village where they had lived in her early childhood, where there were people she called uncle and godfather. This was where her adoption only reinforced the problems connected with her adoptive parents' emigration, because here in the country where Marisol had been born, they had no larger adoptive family to offer her. Clearly, grandparents, uncles, and cousins play a necessary role in the distribution of affection, and if they do not exist as such, one must invent them; yet curiously enough, the invented relatives in Marisol's case were considered "second-rate" and consequently more precarious, less "durable."

Marisol had been alarmed when she learned that her mother was planning to sell the house in the village, a house the father had given her. Marisol expressed anxiety in the face of the power wielded by mothers; they can get rid of the things men give them and do whatever they like with them, and with children, too. She thought that her natural mother had been the one to give her up for adoption and that her father had not objected because there was no one to look after her. Yet on other occasions she said that it was men who got women pregnant and women who have to give the babies away and be disgraced: she felt sorry for the mother she never knew.

She recalled a "terrible accident" where "a girl was run over by a truck; she was covered with blood and no one wanted to take her."

Time and time again, in different ways, Marisol returned to the theme of not being accepted, which was burdensome to her. Feeling that she had not been accepted by her natural parents prevented her from accepting the mother who had indeed accepted her. She saw her mother as someone who had interfered, as if she had stepped between Marisol and her "real" mother. Marisol felt that her relationships with others could not "last long"; each relationship would always get to the point where they "couldn't take me" because she used her deprivation aggressively, as a secret, and tried to act superior to others, with the result that others in the end rejected her. She said that other people did the same bad things she did but their relations with others lasted longer because they have "real parents."

In one of her frequent altercations with her mother, Marisol asked, "Why didn't you pick another girl to adopt and leave me alone?" She immediately regretted having said this and burst out crying; confused and desperate, she went to kiss her mother.

After this episode, Marisol presented abundant material about various people who "were not grateful for the help they get or the gifts they receive" because they feel too much hatred for being dispossessed, abandoned, or incapable of something—like herself and her two mothers: the first was not "grateful enough" for the pregnancy to keep the child, and the second was ungrateful toward the "father's gifts," the house, his semen, which she could not keep for being sterile.

It was only after a long process of exploration that these fantasies were worked through in the transference relation. Marisol learned to cope with the terror of being "too annoying" for the analyst and the fear of being expelled from analysis because the analyst "couldn't put up with her." She was able to improve her relation to her mother, admit that her father was far from ideal, and accept both despite their defects. This made her feel that she herself could be accepted as well, despite her hostility and resentment.

After an arduous journey she could "adopt them" and "be grateful for what they gave her" while admitting, painful as it was, that she had once had other parents, whom she had lost. Similarly, the immigrant needs not only to be adopted by the new

210

country but to be able to adopt it in turn and mourn for the country of origin he has lost.

In Marisol's history, the problems were overlapping since her natural parents were from her native country whereas her adoptive parents were themselves "adopted children" of their daughter's country. This fact caused them unconsciously to use their daughter as an adoptive mother, reversing the roles and further complicating an already conflictive situation.

Josef

Josef, an adopted boy, came to analysis at the age of fourteen with behavioral problems much more serious and glaring than Marisol's. Josef had not been "deceived" about the fact that he was adopted, but other factors associated with migrations weighed heavily in his personal history.

Josef was born in Israel, a place where it is not out of the ordinary to be the child of immigrants. What made his case unusual was that Josef's adoptive parents were cultured, rich, blonde Europeans, whereas everything about Josef, a lean, dark, good-looking boy, betrayed his North African, low-social-class origins. No one believed him when he said his last name because of the physical disparities between his parents and him. He felt like "the servant's son" and as such cultivated permanent resentment which he expressed in persistent clashes, both direct and indirect, with his father. He provoked scenes, got himself expelled from schools, and stole things while leaving clues behind, as if to make trouble for his father, a socially prominent man.

Adoption for Josef had meant not only migration from one set of parents to another but also from one environment and social class to another. He could not adjust to the change. He liked to walk through seedy neighborhoods among people of the worst sort, imagining that any one of them could be his father or mother.

He felt sorry for his original parents, developing the belief that he had been stolen from them because they were poor; he saw

himself as the future settler of their claims. However, he manically denied the deep pain he felt when in his analysis he mentioned fantasies of his parents copulating "wildly" with no concern for the "shrimp" about to be born, whom they could give
away or throw on the garbage heap.

All Josef's repressed hatred for the parents who had abandoned
him was projected onto those who had taken him in and raised
him. He stole from them, just as he felt that he himself had been
stolen from and deprived of his true parents.

As in Marisol's case, the greatest conflict came out against the
parent of the same sex, with whom he wanted to—but could
not—identify. His Oedipal jealousy was of a nearly delirious
nature. Whereas Marisol had said, "Why does my mother interfere in my relationship with my father?" Josef cried, "What is
that man doing in this house? When he's not here we're a lot
better off."

Not surprisingly, Josef's treatment was highly problematic. In
the early stages he tirelessly attacked, belittled, and ridiculed the
analyst, whom he experienced as "my father's accomplice,"
"bourgeois," "an intellectual who doesn't know what life is all
about," someone who "steals money from my parents," and so
on. It was only after some time had passed that he could see,
among other things, that what he most reproached his adopted
father for was not being his real father. This was part of his "family
romance": he loved the idea that he might be the natural son of
the union of his father with another woman; in this way he recovered in fantasy at least one of his parents and thus mitigated his
feeling of loss and helplessness.

It is not mere coincidence that the two cases chosen as examples
for their interest and wealth of material are cases of pubescent
children. This age is always difficult, especially for adopted children. The reenacted Oedipal conflict has a greater possibility of
being fulfilled with adopted children; the incestuous desires the
child feels are, and yet are not, incest; and their struggle to acquire
a sense of identity is fiercer and more painful. They must mourn

the loss of the loved Oedipal object, the loss of their child's body, the loss of their childhood parents, and also the loss of the "other parents" whom they have not known but have both idealized and hated; finally, they must mourn their own abandonment.

One must not forget that Oedipus himself was an adopted child, although he did not know it; and in the story he actually kills the father who had sentenced him to death, a death which was replaced by exile (migration) and his subsequent adoption. Adoption saved Oedipus's life but could not save him from the tragedy derived from the conditions of his birth.

Surrendering a Child

Every adoption is preceded by an explicit or implicit surrender of paternity by the parents. In some countries children can be adopted legally only if the mother executes a formal waiver; however, this does contain the proviso that she has the right to reconsider her decision up to six months after the adoption.

In Spain and perhaps in other places, it is common for cultural and socioeconomic reasons to give children up temporarily or permanently to other family members who function as de facto adoptive parents. Often the overt reason is emotional or physical incapacity of the parents which makes cohabitation difficult or a change of environment advisable. In some cases, the principal motive for surrendering a child is financial: large families cannot support all the children, or the parents must emigrate to look for work or better living conditions, and the children are left in relatives' care, sometimes for many years. But in most cases the unconscious motivation lies in the sense of guilt that many mothers feel toward their own mothers (or childless sisters), which makes it impossible for them to take on the maternal role; they give their children to their mothers in an attempt to placate these fearsome figures and soothe their own persecutory guilt, as though performing an act of sacrifice to pacify the wrath of primitive gods.

For parents to give up their children in infancy or for children

to be abandoned is a relatively frequent occurrence and is generally not considered a problem or reason for further treatment;
such cases are seen in private practice as well as in hospitals.
Rather, the circumstance of adoption usually surfaces at a later
point if the patient's history and its consequences come under
scrutiny.

Drs. J. Rallo, R. Corominas, M. Samanes, and F. Acosta of the
Child Psychiatry Division of the Jiménez Díaz Foundation, who
routinely treat cases of this type, have published a study of the
motivations behind adoption (1972); their conclusions concur
with those offered above. Their study provides many graphic
examples. In one instance, they actually observed the transfer of
a baby from daughter to mother after a number of interviews
with the parties. To describe it briefly, a middle-aged woman under
treatment for a second bout of depression following the death of
her fourteen-year-old son was very aggressive and reproachful
toward her grown daughters, one of whom was pregnant. Some
time later the pregnant daughter, who had given birth to a son,
sought treatment for symptoms of acute depression. Her condition developed regressively, and she had severe anxiety attacks,
reminiscent of puerperal psychosis (thoughts of killing her son,
wanting him to disappear, suicidal fantasies, and so forth). Since
she was not in condition to care for her baby, she surrendered
him to her mother, who assumed the role of new mother with
visible satisfaction.

This case, although extreme, is abundantly clear. The dynamic
at work is often seen in more disguised forms: a dominant and
aggressive mother in intense rivalry with her daughter makes her
feel guilty for any sign of adulthood and independence—and
therefore, any sign of sexuality and maternity—and induces in
her such a high degree of dependency and submission that the
daughter ends up surrendering her own children. This predicament is also marked, as one may suppose, by a weak, absent
father who cannot confront the mother. The surrender of the
child may occur at varying ages, depending on the circumstances,
and may be either temporary or permanent. What aftereffects

does the surrender have? Might it also be considered a specific type of migration? We believe so. Perhaps surrender of this kind is more properly a migration than an adoption per se since both families (as, in the case of the emigrant, both the original and adopted countries) are known to the child, and in some cases, after some time has elapsed, a return is possible.

The surrendered child is not deceived as the adopted child is, and he does not struggle with the ghosts of undiscovered origins. Yet he will not be free of the feeling that his parents abandoned him or that he was different from his brothers and sisters (if he had any) or from other children. He, too, experiences the transfer as an expulsion from his house or as an "escape." He will not be able to avoid feeling a double allegiance and double loyalty, and within himself the families will be in opposition to each other as he constantly compares them and idealizes one to the detriment of the other.

The surrendered child frequently displaces and discharges his hostility and resentment against the people he lives with while idealizing the absent figures. He protests, using the many recourses children have at their disposal, and he displays behavioral problems such as arguments, tantrums, whims, theft; he attacks those around him by means of complaints or criticism while praising the "other" family and trying to provoke rivalry between the two by scheming and lying; alternatively, his reactions may become manifest physically, through anorexia, vomiting, enuresis, and so on.

If both families respond to these provocations or use the child to settle their personal conflicts, rivalries, and guilt over the surrender—the parents, for having abandoned the child; the adoptive parents for fantasizing that they stole him—matters will become all the more entangled for the child, who will be uncomfortable and confused.

Furthermore, it is not unusual, however paradoxical it seems, for adopted children who return to their biological parents to go through a stage of directing anger against them and being homesick for the lost adopted home. A child who returns to his parents' home after they have given him away is not the same child he would have been if he had not gone away, nor are the parents the same.

The nature of an emigrant's return to his home country is as variable as the subject's personality, the duration of the absence, the many motives for returning, and the circumstances of the return, as well as his success or failure in accomplishing the objectives of the original migration. Yet the inescapable fact is that no return is solely a return; it is a new migration, and as such implies all the fears and hopes that characterize migration. Those who return are not the same people they were when they left, and the place they return to is not the same place.

BY WAY OF AN EPILOGUE

One never goes back, one always goes toward.

REFERENCES

Achard de Demaria, L., and J. P. Galeano Massera. 1982. "Vicisitudes del inmigrante." *Rev. de Psicoanálisis* 40:2, 1984.

Anzieu, D. 1976. "Narciso. La envoltura sonora del sí mismo." *Nouvelle Revue de Psychanalyse* 13 (Spring).

Balint, M. 1959. *Thrills and Regressions*. London, Hogarth and the Institute of Psycho-Analysis.

Benedetti, M. 1982. *Primavera con una esquina rota*. Madrid, Alfaguara.

Benveniste, E. 1969. "El lenguaje y la experiencia humana." In *Problemas del lenguaje*. Buenos Aires, Sudamericana.

Berenstein, I. 1982. *Psicoanálisis de la estructura familiar. Del destino a la significación*. Barcelona, Paidos-Ibérica.

Bick, E. 1968. "The Experience of Skin in Early Object Relations." *Int. J. of Psycho-Anal*. 49: 2–3.

Bion, W. R. 1962. *Learning from Experience*. London, W. Heinemann.

———. 1963. *Elements of Psychoanalysis*. London, W. Heinemann.

———. 1965. *Transformations*. London, W. Heinemann.

———. 1970. *Attention and Interpretation*. London, Tavistock.

Bowlby, J. 1960. "Separation Anxiety." *Int. J. Psycho-Anal*. 41.

Calvo, F. 1977. *Qué es ser emigrante?* Barcelona, La Gaya Ciencia.

Canetti, E. 1980. *La lengua absuelta*. Barcelona, Muchnik.

Chomsky, N. 1965. *Aspects of the Theory of Syntax*. Cambridge, MIT Press.

———. 1969. *Lingüística cartesiana*. Madrid, Gredos.

Delibes, M. 1958. *Diario de un emigrante*. Barcelona, Destino, 1980.

Dellarossa, G. D. de. 1978. "The Professional of Immigrant Descent." *Int. J. of Psych*. 59, part 3.

Denford, S. 1981. "Going Away." *Int. Review of Psycho-Analysis* 8, part 3.

De Saussure, F. (1961). *Curso de Lingüística General*. 5th edition. Buenos Aires, Losada.

Donoso, J. 1981. *El jardín de al lado*. Barcelona, Seix Barral.

Ekstein, R. 1977. Personal correspondence.

Erikson, E. 1956. "The Problem of Ego Identity." *J. Am. Psycho-Anal. Ass.* 4.

———. 1959. *Childhood and Society.* Boston, Little, Brown.

Ferrer, S. L. de. 1958. "Migración y regresión." *Revista Médica de Córdoba* 46.

Freud, S. 1895. "Studies in Hysteria." S.E. 2.

———. 1896. "Further Remarks on the Neuro-Psychoses of Defense." S.E. 3.

———. 1920. *Beyond the Pleasure Principle.* S.E. 18.

———. 1926. *Inhibitions, Symptoms and Anxiety.* S.E. 20.

———. 1926. "Address to the Society of B'nai B'rith." S.E. 20.

———. 1938. "Letter to Max Eitington." In *Letters of Sigmund Freud.* Selected and edited by Ernst L. Freud. New York, Basic Books, 1960.

Garza-Guerrero, A. C. 1974. "Culture Shock: Its Mourning and the Vicissitudes of Identity." *J. Am. Psychoanal. Ass.* 22:2.

Green, A. 1975. "The Analyst, Symbolization and Absence in the Analytic Setting." *Int. J. Psycho-Anal.* 50.

Greenacre, Ph. 1958. "Early Physical Determinants in the Development of Sense of Identity." *J. Am. Psychoanal. Ass.* 6.

Greenson, R. 1950. "The Mother Tongue and the Mother." *Int. J. of Psycho-Anal.* 31.

Grinberg, L. 1963. *Culpa y depresión.* Buenos Aires, Paidos. Edición española: Madrid, Alianza Universidad Textos, 1983.

———. 1978. "The 'Razor's Edge' in Depression and Mourning." *Int. J. Psycho-Anal.* 59, pp. 245–54.

Grinberg, L., et al. 1967. "Función del soñar y clasificación clínica de los sueños en el proceso analítico." *Rev. de Psicoanálisis* 24.

Grinberg, L., and R. Grinberg. 1971. *Identidad y cambio.* Buenos Aires, Kargieman; Barcelona, Paidos-Ibérica, 1980.

Grinberg, R. 1965. "Migración e identidad." Paper presented at the Asociación Psicoanalítica Argentina.

———. 1980. "Migración e identidad." In *Identidad y cambio*, by L. Grinberg and R. Grinberg, Barcelona, Paidos-Ibérica, 3d ed.

———. 1982. "La migración y la cesión: dos migraciones específicas." *Rev. de la A.P.D.E.B.A.* 4:1.

Jacques, E. 1966. "La crisis de la edad media de la vida" (Mid-Life Crisis). *Rev. de Psic.* 23:4.

Jakobson, R. 1963. *Essais de lingüistique générale.* Paris, Ed. de Minuit.

Joseph, B. 1978. "Towards the Experience of Psychic Pain." In *Do I*

Dare Disturb The Universe? A memorial to Wilfred R. Bion. Ed. by
J. S. Grotstein-Beverly Hills, Caesura Press. 1981.

Kaës, R., et al. 1959. *Crise, Rupture et Dépassement.* Paris, Dunod.

Kafka, F. 1927. *Amerika.*

———. (1945): *The Castle*

Kijac, M., y Funtowicz 1981. "The Syndrome of the Survivor of
Extreme Situations." Paper presented at the 33d *Congress* Psicoanal.
Int., Helsinki.

Klein, M. 1929. "Infantile Anxiety Situations Reflected in a Work of
Art and in the Creative Impulse." In *Contributions to
Psychoanalysis, 1921–1945.* London, Hogarth, 1950.

———. 1932. *El psicoanálisis de niños.* Buenos Aires, Asoc. Psic.
Argentina y El Ateneo, 1948.

———. 1955. "On Identification." In *New Directions in Psycho-
Analysis.* Ed. M. Klein, P. Heimann, R. E. Money-Kyrle. London,
Tavistock.

———. 1963. "On the Sense of Loneliness." In *On Envy and
Gratitude and Other Works. 1946–1963.* London, Hogarth and the
Institute of Psycho-Analysis, 1975.

Lacan, J. 1953. "Discours de J. Lacan dans les Actes du Congrès de
Rome." La Psychoanalyse.

Liberman, A. 1982. Personal correspondence.

Liberman, D. 1971. *Lingüística, interacción comunicativa y proceso
psicoanalítico.* Buenos Aires, Galerna. I.

Mahler, M. 1971. "A Study of the Separation-Individuation Process."
In *The Psychoanalytic Study of the Child* 26. New Haven, Yale
Univ. Press, 1974.

Mann, T. 1941. *Herman Hesse–Thomas Mann. Correspondence.*
Barcelona: Muchnik, 1977.

Meltzer, D. 1973. "El mutismo en el autismo infantil, la esquizofrenia
y los estados maníaco-depresivos: la correlación entre la
psicopatología clínica y la lingüística." *Rev. de Psicoanálisis* 30:
3–4.

Menges, L. J. 1959. "Geschiktheid voor emigratic. Een onderzock naar
enkele psychologische aspecten der emigrabiliteit" (Adequacy for
migrating. An investigation of some psychological aspects of
migration). Diss., Univ. Leiden, The Hague.

Morris, Ch. 1962. *Signos, lenguaje y conducta.* Buenos Aires, Losada.

Moses, R. 1978. "Adult Psychic Trauma. The Question of Early

Predisposition and Some Detailed Mechanisms." *Int. J. Psycho-Anal.*
59: 2–3.

Niederland, W. 1968. "Clinical Observations on the 'Survivor
Syndrome.'" *Int. J. Psycho-Anal.* 49.

Pollock, G. 1967. Discussion in the Kris Study Group of New York.

Prieto, L. J. 1967. *Mensajes y señales.* Barcelona, Seix Barral.

Racker, H. 1952. "Aportación al psicoanálisis de la música." *Rev. de
Psicoanálisis* 9.

Rallo, J., R. Corominas, M. Samanes, F. Acosta. 1972. "La cesión, una
forma especial de adopción." *Boletín de la Fundación Jiménez Díaz.*

Rank, O. 1924. *The Trauma of Birth.*

Rodríguez Pérez, J. F. 1982. Personal correspondence with authors.

Ruesh, J., and W. Kees. (1956): *Nonverbal Communication.* Berkeley,
University of California Press.

Sánchez Ferlosio, R. 1983. Newspaper article, *El País* (Madrid), August
26, 1983.

Schaff, A. 1969. "Lenguaje y realidad." In *Problems del lenguaje.*
Buenos Aires, Sudamericana.

Singer, I. B. 1972. *Enemigos. Una historia de amor.* Barcelona, Plaza y
Janés.

Stengel, E. 1939. "On learning a new language." *Int. J. Psycho-Anal.*
20.

Tausk, V. 1919. "On the Origin of the Influence Machine in
Schizophrenia." *Psychoanal. Quarterly* 2.

Thom, R. 1976. "Crise et Catastrophe." *Communications* 25.

Ticho, G. 1971. "Cultural aspects of transference and
countertransference." *Bull. Menninger Clinic,* 35.

Torres, M. 1983. Newspaper article, *El País* (Madrid), December 4,
1983.

Winnicott, D. 1955. "Metapsychological and Clinical Aspects of
Regression within the Psychoanalytical Set-up." *Int. J. Psycho-Anal.*
36.

———. 1958. "The Capacity to Be Alone." In *The Maturational
Processes and the Facilitating Environment.* London, Hogarth and
the Institute of Psychoanalysis, 1965.

———. 1971. *Playing and Reality.* London, Tavistock.

INDEX

References in italic refer to
material in case studies.

Abandonment, feelings of: in
  adopted child, *202, 203, 205,*
  211; in second-generation
  immigrant, *171–72, 173;* in
  surrendered child, *214*
Abraham (biblical character),
  migration of, 5–6
Acceptance, *208–09*
Achievement, *168, 170. See also*
  Manic defense
Acosta, F., 213
Adolescence: immigration during,
  127–28; as migration, 197;
  peer group and, 128; reaffirmation of sexual identity in,
  197–98
Adoption: case study of, *202–10,*
  210–12; as migration,
  200–15; motivations behind,
  212–13; vs. surrendering a
  child, 212–14
Age, 113–28; ease of migration
  and, 179; mental health of
  emigrants and, 126. *See also*
  Childhood migration; Development, human
Aggression: control of, and
  migration, 195; mass social,
  Holocaust as, 153; in survivor
  syndrome, *151, 152*
Alpha functions, and dreams,

140–41
Anal-muscular maturation stage,
  123–25
Anxiety, 2–3; catastrophic, 11;
  desire to leave and, 59–60; in
  migratory process, 87; psychotic states and, 88; regression and, in newly arrived
  immigrants, 75–76; return
  home and, 187; separation, 77.
  See also Depressive anxiety;
  Disorienting anxiety; Paranoid
  anxiety; Persecutory anxiety
Anzieu, D., 104, 192
Argentina, immigrants in,
  166–75
Arrival, 74–80
Automatic anxiety. *See* Catastrophic anxiety

Babel myth, 8–9
Balint, M., 21
Bateson, G., 137–38
Benedetti, M., 158, 159, 165, 180
Benveniste, E., 99
Berenstein, I., 95, 134, 141, 153
Bick, E., 47, 191
Bion, W. R., 3; becoming O and,
  65, 66; contained–container
  relation and, 81–82; pain and,
  64; psychosis and, 138–39
Birth: Eden myth and, 5; as first
  migration, 5, 191–93; trauma
  of, and response to migration,